EASTERN FRONT FROM

WEHRMACHT COMBAT REPORTS

THE RUSSIAN FRONT

Edited and introduced
by Bob Carruthers

Pen & Sword
MILITARY

This edition published in 2013 by
Pen & Sword Military
An imprint of
Pen & Sword Books Ltd
47 Church Street
Barnsley
South Yorkshire
S70 2AS

First published in Great Britain in 2011 in digital format by
Coda Books Ltd.

Copyright © Coda Books Ltd, 2012
Published under licence by Pen & Sword Books Ltd.

ISBN 978 1 78159 214 4

A CIP catalogue record for this book is
available from the British Library

Printed and bound by CPI Group (UK) Ltd, Croydon, CR0 4YY

Pen & Sword Books Ltd incorporates the Imprints of Pen & Sword Aviation, Pen &
Sword Family History, Pen & Sword Maritime, Pen & Sword Military, Pen & Sword
Discovery, Pen & Sword Politics, Pen & Sword Atlas, Pen & Sword Archaeology,
Wharncliffe Local History, Wharncliffe True Crime, Wharncliffe Transport, Pen & Sword
Select, Pen & Sword Military Classics, Leo Cooper, The Praetorian Press, Claymore
Press, Remember When, Seaforth Publishing and Frontline Publishing

For a complete list of Pen & Sword titles please contact
PEN & SWORD BOOKS LIMITED
47 Church Street, Barnsley, South Yorkshire, S70 2AS, England
E-mail: enquiries@pen-and-sword.co.uk
Website: www.pen-and-sword.co.uk

CONTENTS

INTRODUCTION

I N A CAREER marked by a litany of mistakes, surely Hitler's biggest mistake of all was to drag a reluctant US into World War II. Even after the Japanese attack on Pearl Harbour Hitler still had the option to keep the US out of the war. In a typical act of delusion Hitler, on 11th December 1941, declared war on the largest industrial nation on earth. From that moment onwards the fate of Nazi Germany was sealed. It took some months to awake the sleeping giant, but once the US juggernaut began to roll the end result of World War II was never in question.

While the US was busy assembling its new armies, navies and air forces, the US Intelligence Service was already beginning to gather intelligence on its new enemy. This information was collated and disseminated to the troops who needed it, in the form of two main monthly intelligence bulletins. These were Tactical and Technical Trends which first appeared in June 1942 and the Intelligence Bulletin which began to appear from September 1942 onwards.

The main focus for the US was initially on the war with Japan and a great majority of the early reports are concerned with the war in the Pacific. However, as America began to come up to speed US forces were soon engaged in North Africa, followed by Sicily, Italy and finally Northern Europe. As the war progressed the requirement for good intelligence of German battlefield tactics became more and more important and in consequence there are more and more reports of German fighting techniques available to us. The vast majority of those reports concerned the fighting in Russia and it is those reports which form the bulk of what you are about to read here.

The material for the two US intelligence journals was originally collected from British combat reports, German newspapers, captured German documents, German training manuals and Soviet sources. As such the quality of much of what was printed was highly variable, some reports are very accurate, while in others, the precision of the

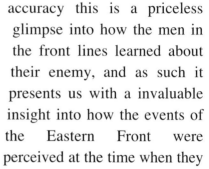

information is questionable to say the least, but that's what makes these reports so fascinating. Regardless of the overall accuracy this is a priceless glimpse into how the men in the front lines learned about their enemy, and as such it presents us with a invaluable insight into how the events of the Eastern Front were perceived at the time when they actually unfolded. The reports also provide us with a host of information concerning the minor aspects of the thousands of tactical combats being waged day in and day out which expand our knowledge of the realities of the fighting in Russia.

Thank you for buying this book. I hope you enjoy reading these long forgotten reports as much as I enjoyed discovering them and collating them for you. Other volumes in this series are already in preparation and I hope you will decide to join me in other discoveries as the series develops.

Bob Carruthers

1. SOME BASIC GERMAN TACTICS

Tactical and Technical Trends

The following are summaries of certain phases of basic German tactics.

a. The Meeting Engagement

(1) A meeting engagement means that a commander dispenses with preliminary preparations, and deploys straight into battle. Careful coordination and a determination to succeed on the part of all concerned will compensate for the absence of preliminary preparations.

(2) A commander will not commit himself to a meeting engagement unless either:

    (a) he feels that his troops and leadership are superior to that of the enemy (this does not necessarily mean a numerical superiority) or;

    (b) he would, by waiting to launch a deliberate attack, sacrifice ground which he cannot afford to lose.

(3) Sound tactical decisions in the initial stages are essential. Mistakes cannot afterwards be rectified. The worst mistake of all is hesitation.

(4) The advance guard will delay the enemy and seize important positions, e.g., for artillery OPs. It may therefore:

    (a) attack with a limited objective;

    (b) defend its existing positions;

    (c) withdraw to more favorable positions. (Withdrawal is likely to hinder the deployment of the main body.)

(5) The main body will deploy immediately. To wait for further information in the hope of clarifying the situation is wrong. Time will be lost and lost time can never be regained. The time available determines whether the commander should concentrate his troops before launching them to the attack, or launch them on their tasks as they become available.

(6) The meeting engagement will normally take the form of a frontal attack by the advance guard, combined with one or more enveloping attacks by the main body.

b. The Deliberate Attack

(1) The object of the attack is to surround and destroy the enemy.

(2) A strong, rapid, enveloping attack can be decisive, provided that it really gets to grips with the enemy, and that the enemy is pinned down by frontal pressure which will be exercised mainly by fire.

(3) Enveloping forces must move in depth if they are not to be themselves outflanked. All enveloping attacks ultimately become frontal.

(4) In all attacks, the commander will select a "Schwerpunkt" or point of main effort, where the bulk of his forces will be employed. ("A commander without a Schwerpunkt is like a man without character.") The considerations when choosing this point are:

(a) Weaknesses in the enemy defense;

(b) Suitability of the ground for cooperation of all arms, but especially for tanks;

(c) Avenues of approach;

(d) Possibilities of supporting fire, especially by artillery.

(5) Boundaries and objectives are allotted to attacking units. This does not mean, however, that a unit must cover the whole ground within its boundaries with troops. It will choose within its boundaries the best line, or lines of advance, and dispose its troops accordingly. A Schwerpunkt battalion can be allotted about 450 yards of front, while a battalion which is attacking in the non-Schwerpunkt area may be given 1,000 yards or more.

(6) An attack on a narrow front must have sufficient forces at its disposal to widen the breach, maintain its impetus, and protect the flanks of the penetration. Once an attack has been launched, it must drive straight on, regardless of opposition, to its objective. It is wrong for the leading attacking troops to turn aside to deal with threats to their flanks. This is the task of the troops which are following them.

(7) A breakthrough must be in sufficient depth to prevent the enemy from establishing new positions in rear. The breakthrough cannot be successful until the enemy artillery positions are captured. This is the special task of the tanks.

(8) As soon as enemy resistance weakens at any point, all available fire and forces must be concentrated to insure the success of the breakthrough.

(9) Continuous artillery support is essential. Therefore artillery must be kept well forward.

c. The Pursuit

(1) If the enemy is able to withdraw under cover of a rearguard, the attack has failed. He must then be pursued.

(2) The object of the pursuing forces will be to encircle and destroy the enemy. Infantry and artillery alone are not sufficient for this.

(3) Aircraft will attack defiles on his line of retreat, and motorized elements will endeavor to pierce his front and envelop his flanks. A Schwerpunkt and clear orders are just as necessary in this operation as in any other.

(4) The task of the pursuing forces is to interfere with, and if possible stop, the enemy's withdrawal, so that he can be dealt with by the slower-moving infantry and artillery which will be following up.

(5) Troops pursuing the enemy may find themselves in great difficulties owing to the speed with which they move and the exposed positions in which they may find themselves. They must be prepared for this, and must rely on aircraft and the slower-moving infantry and artillery to get them out of their difficulties in due course.

d. Defense

(1) A Schwerpunkt is as necessary in the defense as it is in the attack.

(2) A defensive position is only of value if the enemy must attack, or if it is so strong that the enemy is afraid to attack it. If the enemy can avoid a defensive position by passing round its flanks, it has no value.

(3) Defensive positions will be held to the last man.

(4) Essentials of a defensive position are:

    (a) A good field of fire for all arms, but especially the artillery;

    (b) Good observation;

    (c) Concealment;

    (d) Natural protection against tanks;

    (e) The ability to concentrate the fire of all weapons in front of the main line of resistance.

(5) The defensive position is divided into covering force, outposts, and a main position. The forward edge of the latter is known as the main line of resistance.

(6) The task of the covering force is to deny good observation points to the enemy and to hinder his advance. They will be approximately 6,000 to 8,000 yards in front of the main position. Mines and obstacles will be used to strengthen the position of the covering force. The covering force must not expose themselves to the danger of being overwhelmed. They will be withdrawn at a definite time. They will normally consist of small mobile forces. Their principal task is to force the enemy to deploy.

(7) The outposts are responsible for the immediate protection of the main position. Their tasks are:

    (a) To prevent the enemy from surprising the forces holding the main position;

    (b) To mislead the enemy as long as possible as to the dispositions and situation of the main position;

    (c) To protect advanced OP's.

They will be withdrawn when the situation makes it necessary. They are normally 2,000 to 3,000 yards in front of the main position.

(8) The main position must be defended in depth. This consideration is paramount. Areas and not lines will be defended. If the enemy should succeed in penetrating a position, he must be faced by a series of defended areas, mutually supporting one another by fire, so that in the end he collapses under the concentrated fire directed at him. A battalion will defend from 800 to 2,000 yards.

(9) The withdrawal of both covering forces and outposts must be carefully planned, to avoid masking the fire of the main position.

(10) Penetration must be met by immediate local counterattacks with limited objectives, carried out by small parties of infantry, and if possible against the enemy's flanks. Unless tanks are available, a deliberate counterattack will succeed only if carried out by superior forces and as a surprise against one or both flanks of the enemy penetration. Like any other deliberate attack, it requires preparation.

e. Village Fighting

Troops are too easily attracted to villages. These give some cover from fire, but also draw it, and may become traps.

(1) Attack

    (a) In attack, villages should be bypassed if possible. The enemy in the village must, however, be pinned down, chiefly by artillery fire, when this is happening.

    (b) If they must be attacked, heavy supporting fire is needed on the nearer edge, especially on isolated buildings and small groups of houses.

    (c) Leading troops will avoid the streets, and fight through backyards and gardens to the far end of the village. These troops are difficult to control and support, and must therefore operate in small independent groups. Their tasks must be accurately laid down, and each group must have its own supporting weapons.

    (d) Reserves must move close behind these leading groups, as they may easily get into difficulties.

(2) Defense

    (a) Well-built villages make good strongpoints.

    (b) Their edges are shell traps. The main defended line should therefore be either inside or outside, not on the edges.

    (c) If a village is favorably situated, it should be turned into a strongpoint organized in depth. The irregular shape of its approaches should provide ample opportunities for flanking fire.

    (d) Villages are especially useful as antitank positions.

Reserves must be held in readiness outside the village to deal with the enemy's probable attempts to bypass it.

2. GERMAN NOTES ON STREET FIGHTING

Tactical and Technical Trends, No. 17, January 28th 1943

In view of the importance of the strong internal defense of towns under siege as demonstrated in Russia, the following notes on street fighting has particular significance at this time. The notes which follow are taken from a German handbook dated January 1939.

It is of interest to compare this article on German methods with British notes on street fighting contained in the next article.

a. Attack

(1) Towns will be surrounded, and water, power and gas cut off.

(2) The enemy-occupied area will be attacked with the object of dividing it. These areas will then be isolated into as many pockets as possible, so as to deny the enemy freedom of movement.

(3) Attacking parties should move in the same direction along parallel streets. Parties moving in opposite directions create confusion and cause friendly troops to fire on each other.

(4) High buildings with commanding positions will be taken whenever possible.

(5) Flanking attacks should not be attempted.

(6) Troops should advance along both sides of the street, keeping close to the houses.

(7) Parties should also attack across roofs, and from house to house.

(8) In the streets, men will be detailed to watch roofs, windows, crossings, etc., on the side of the street opposite them.

(9) Single light machine guns can be moved along streets to open direct fire on points of resistance. To destroy large buildings, smaller guns than 150-mm are useless.

(10) Tanks will not be brought into towns.

(11) Areas occupied will be systematically searched.

b. Defense

(1) The enemy must not be able to pick out the main defense areas. These should therefore not be on the edge of the town, where strongpoints only should be used to threaten the enemy's flank.

(2) Important buildings must be defended from positions outside, and not from the building itself.

(3) The enemy should be driven into pockets, and any advanced elements cut off by sudden flank attacks.

(4) All windows will be left open so that the enemy will not know out of which window fire may come, and thus he will be unable to concentrate his own fire.

(5) Do not fire from the window-sill, but from a point as far back as possible.

(6) Remove tiles to make loopholes. Good positions can also be obtained behind chimneys.

(7) Barricades must be properly erected and well covered with fire. Use all means possible to keep streets illuminated at night.

3. THE FORCING OF THE NAREW RIVER CROSSING

Tactical and Technical Trends,
No. 27, June 17th 1943

The following translation from a German military review gives an account of the German crossing of the Narew River at a point about 100 miles northeast of Warsaw on June 25, 1941. The account illustrates very concretely the German methods employed in a small tactical operation. Of special importance in the success of this action were: The effective combined use of the various arms (particularly supporting artillery); the flexibility of control, which permitted rapid adjustment of tactical plans to meet a changing situation; and, finally, the offensive spirit that characterized the whole operation.

The Vorausabteilung (advanced detachment) is to be distinguished from the Vorhut (advance guard) and operates in front of the latter. It is formed to carry out specific tasks connected, at least partly, with combat reconnaissance. Its size and composition are flexible. In the action described below, the Vorausabteilung is converted into an Angriffsgruppe (attack group), prior to the general attack.

The translation follows.

THE GERMAN PLAN OF ATTACK FOR JUNE 25

The 499th Infantry Regiment, reinforced, advancing by forced marches, had supported the advanced detachment (Vorausabteilung) of the division in its defensive engagement with enemy* tanks attacking west of Rajsk. [*"Enemy," of course from the German viewpoint. Throughout the translation "enemy" has reference to the Russians.] On the evening of June 24, the most advanced elements of the regiment had reached the Orlanka crossing at Chraboly without any important contact with the enemy. Orders were issued for the regiment to advance the next morning on Ryboly, located north of the Narew. It was assumed that the enemy would evacuate the

Orlanka sector and withdraw behind the Narew in the direction of Bialystok (about 15 miles north of Ryboly).

An advanced detachment (Vorausabteilung) for the regiment was formed, consisting principally of the 9th Bicycle Company, a platoon of engineers (Pioniere), and an assault gun platoon [probably two 75-mm self-propelled guns.] This detachment was to assemble at Banki at 0600, proceed by way of Rajsk and the Orlanka bridge at Chraboly, take possession of the Narew crossing 3 kilometers southwest of Ryboly, and keep this crossing open for the regiment coming up from the rear. The regiment was to follow the advanced detachment in such a way that the advance guard consisting of the 3d Battalion (less the 9th Bicycle Company), one platoon of light infantry howitzers, one anti- tank platoon and one cavalry squad,† was to reach the hill 1 kilometer northeast of the Narew bridge as its first objective, while the main body was following at a distance of 2 kilometers. [† The infantry regiment includes a mounted infantry or a cavalry platoon, consisting of a headquarters and 3 squads.]

Plans for the support of the advance across the Orlanka River were as follows: strong artillery, emplaced at Rajsk, was to be put into readiness for action; from its bridgehead positions at Chraboly, the 2d Battalion (reinforced) was to cover the crossing of the advanced detachment; a battery of assault guns was to be attached to the advanced detachment to cover the advance beyond the Orlanka.

THE ADVANCED DETACHMENT REACHES THE NAREW

The reinforced 9th Bicycle Company (the advanced detachment) arrived at the Chraboly bridgehead at 0730. In as much as the battery of assault guns which had been ordered to the Chraboly bridge had not yet arrived, the company waited. Not until 0815, upon arrival of the assault-gun battery, did the advance detachment start on its march, assault guns ahead.

The forward reconnaissance elements very soon reported that a weak enemy force with machine guns was holding the southern edge of the woods south of the Narew crossing. At 0830, the assault guns, with the most advanced elements of the 9th Company, reached the enemy-occupied edge of the woods and attacked with the object of throwing the enemy across the Narew and seizing the hill north of the crossing.

Effectively supported by the assault guns and the antitank platoon, the company succeeded in throwing the enemy back; a few isolated individual Russian soldiers continued to fight stubbornly in the woods. The main enemy force withdrew to the east and harassed the 9th Company from that direction by means of rifle and machine-gun fire. The company reached the north edge of the woods and found itself before the bridge and the hill to the north, both occupied by the enemy.

Meantime, the advance guard (reinforced 3d Battalion), having been some- what delayed by skirmishes with enemy snipers, had been late in arriving at Rajsk. In order that the march of the main body should not be held up because of this delay, the regimental commander ordered the main body to close up on the advance guard without regard to the prescribed distance of 2 kilometers. The regimental commander went to the northern bank of the Orlanka, where the reinforced 2d Battalion was assembling most of its elements, the remainder continuing to cover the Orlanka crossing. There, the message from the 9th Bicycle Company reached him saying that it was attacking weak enemy forces at the edge of the woods south of the Narew bridge and that the Narew bridge was occupied by stronger enemy units.

Thereupon, all available mobile forces, namely, one engineer company and one antitank company, were rushed ahead in order to reinforce the 9th Company, and were placed under command of the advanced detachment commander. By relentless attack, they were to force the crossing of the Narew and hold the hills beyond as a bridgehead until the arrival of the regiment. .This movement of these reinforcements proceeded with dispatch, and the regimental command post was moved forward to the hill 2.5 kilometers southwest of the Narew bridge.

ESTIMATE OF THE SITUATION (ABOUT 0900)

Here, two reports arrived. First, prisoners stated that the enemy was intending to defend the Narew. Their statements were at first regarded as incorrect, in view of the general estimate of the situation. However, a short time later an air observation report came in that enemy motorized forces were advancing on Zabludow from the northeast; this appeared to confirm the prisoners' statements.

The regimental commander now estimated the situation to be that the enemy was bringing up forces to defend the Narew southwest of Ryboly. He stuck to his plans of seizing the crossing from the enemy by means of a quick grab and decisive attack before the latter could bring up any stronger forces. To effect this plan, the approaching advance guard (3d Battalion) was ordered to attack immediately, from march formation, to the right of the road and to seize the hills and the Narew bridge. The 1st Battalion, which was closely following the 3rd, was to move forward rapidly and get into attacking position on the left flank of the 3d Battalion, with the same missions namely, to seize the hill beyond the river as quickly as possible and hold it.

As for the artillery, one battery was moving to a position east of the new regimental command post; two batteries still were concentrated to the east of Rajsk, ready to open fire. They were to hinder the approach of the enemy motorized forces by means of interdiction fire on Ryboly. A battalion of medium artillery, a liaison officer of which reported to the regimental staff, was to fire on the road south of Ryboly so as to block the enemy's path to the Narew bridge.

THE ENEMY RESISTANCE IS STRONG (0930)

At 0930, the 3d Battalion reached the hilltop at the command post. According to messages reaching the regiment at that time, the situation in front was bad: the enemy had heavily occupied the hills beyond the river and was inflicting severe casualties, by means of rifle, machine-gun, mortar, and artillery fire, on the troops of the advanced detachment.

Thereupon, the regimental commander went forward himself and ascertained that enemy artillery, reckoned at one medium battery, was shelling the road south of the bridge as far as the regimental command post; some rounds even fell into the positions at Chraboly. The sound of battle indicated that the enemy was resisting stubbornly.

In order to force the attack forward, the regimental commander ordered one of the assault gun platoons to push at once to the far bank of the Narew and engage the enemy. Since signal flares, indicating enemy tanks, were now going up from the wooded area south of the bridge, this order was supplemented by special directions to destroy enemy tanks on the far river bank. An additional assault gun platoon received the same orders. The 3d and 1st Battalions were impressed, once more, with the urgent need for a quick advance. Meanwhile, enemy tank concentrations had been reported at Woiszki and in the woods to the south, and were being engaged by the artillery.

At this time, messages were arriving from the advanced detachment saying that fire from enemy artillery, tank guns, heavy mortars, and infantry howitzers in addition to well-aimed rifle fire, was preventing any forward movement. Some elements had got as far as the river; there, however, they had been stopped by enemy machine-gun fire. Consequently, though the assault guns were on the far bank, no infantry or engineers had reached it as yet. Artillery was therefore ordered to engage the enemy on the north bank.

The enemy artillery fire increased; it was estimated at 4 medium and 4 light pieces. Furthermore, it was reported that the enemy was installed in field fortifications on the far bank of the Narew, and that numerous tanks were engaging the attacking force. No report that the 3d Battalion had succeeded in moving forward was forthcoming. Likewise, the report that the assault guns had got across the river, expended their ammunition, and recrossed with more ammunition, could not change the general picture—that a continuation of the attack did not appear to promise success under the methods employed so far. On the contrary, it seemed possible that casualties would be augmented without the objective being reached.

Moreover, it was ascertained that the 1st Battalion had lost much time in its advance by deploying across open terrain arid that it was still lagging behind; early assistance from this battalion was not to be expected. From the commanding hills, the enemy completely enfiladed the river—600 to 1,000 meters wide, level, and devoid of cover. Finally, the avenue of approach (particularly east of the road) was made difficult by extensive pools and stagnant channels, and the attacking force was not familiar with the crossing conditions on the Narew.

PLAN FOR A COORDINATED ATTACK TO FORCE THE NAREW

The plan of attack was based on the only existing possibility, namely, to seize the crossing by surprise, on, under, and beside the bridge. This naturally required some time, as this area in particular was under heavily concentrated fire from rifles, machine guns, rifle grenades, and tanks.

A coordinated attack had to be planned: the 1st Battalion had to come up, deployment of all elements be completed, and preparatory fires by artillery and heavy weapons laid down.

Therefore, oral fragmentary orders were issued to continue the attack only after systematic preparation and after guarantee of the strongest possible artillery support, as well as support by one antitank battalion. The following forces were to prepare for the assault, south of the Narew:

Right Front: 3d Battalion with one L Inf How Plat, one AT Plat, and the 1st AT Co, all attached.

Left Front: 1st Bn with one L Inf How Plat, one Hv Inf How Plat, and the 2d AT Co, all attached.

Angriffsgruppe *[Attack group.]*: The former advanced detachment (Vorausabteilung), with its attached units, in its present position.

Regtl Reserve: 2d Bn with one L Inf How Plat attached. This force was to reconnoiter possibilities for attacking from a position in the western section of the woods northeast of Deniski.

The commanding hills north of the Narew bridge were designated as the next objective of the regiment.

The main mission of the artillery was to support the 3d Battalion and to prepare the attack by smashing the enemy in the fortified positions north of the bridge; furthermore, to smash enemy tank concentrations south of Ryboly, in the woods southeast of Wojszki, and at Wojszki.

A CHANGE OF PLAN TO MEET A CHANGE IN THE SITUATION (1130)

Toward 1130 the situation took a new turn. The aggressive power of the attacking elements was able to accomplish what had not been considered possible in view of the estimated enemy situation, defending as he was a fortified position, with increasing artillery support and strong tank forces held in readiness.

By exploiting the bold forward thrust of the assault guns, elements of the infantry—about 20 men of the 10th Company—and parts of the engineers had succeeded in pushing to the far bank on and under the bridge, forming a bridgehead and thereby initiating a sweeping general attack across the Narew by the attack group.

Toward 1130, the reports from the liaison officers who had been sent to the units then attacking, (the attack group and the 3d Battalion) revealed the following situation:

The liaison officer with the attack group realized, upon his arrival, that there had been a change in the situation since the issuance of the order for a coordinated attack. It now appeared possible for the forward movement to gain sufficient momentum for a successful assault without a coordinated attack. He hurried to take this important news to the regimental commander.

The liaison officer with the 3d Battalion delivered a message from the 3d Battalion Commander indicating that his attack was in progress, some units already had succeeded in pushing across the river, and could not now be stopped. The most advanced infantry was involved in stubborn close combat with the enemy in foxholes and small trenches. If reinforcements could come up soon, the attack was likely to be successful.

It was now imperative to prevent the attack from stalling; this was the moment to press forward with all available strength.

A considerable element of danger was recognized in the fact that,

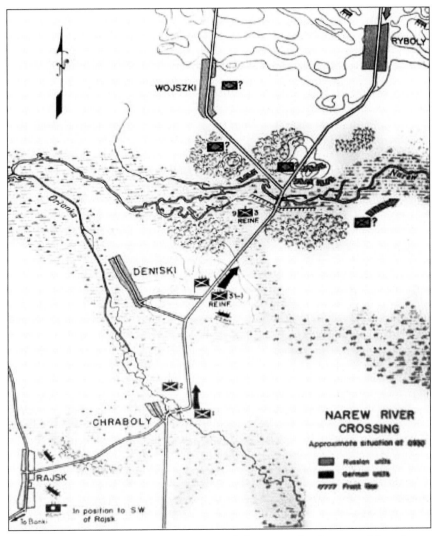

NAREW RIVER
CROSSING

Approximate situation at 0830

Russian units
German units
Front line

during the sweeping continuation of the assault, the attacking force might run into its own artillery fire. However, efforts to shift the fire to a box barrage succeeded in time; later it turned out that the artillery fire had been falling directly in front of the infantry and had greatly facilitated the attack.

The liaison officers with the attacking units were rushed forward with the new and final order to dispense with any preparation for a coordinated attack and to press the attack now in progress, with the hill north of Ryboly as the next objective (3d Battalion to the right of the road, 1st Battalion to the left of the road).

SUCCESS

The regimental command post was moved forward to the hill north of the Narew bridge. This was done at a moment when the most advanced elements, generally speaking, had cleared the enemy positions on the hill to the right of the road. There were one or two dead Russians lying in every foxhole; now and then, shots were still being fired by some individual Russians who obviously had simulated death. Parts of the 3d Battalion turned east so as to clear the grain fields of enemy riflemen; other elements fought their way into the wooded rolling country 500 meters north of the Narew bridge.

Only a few tanks were still resisting; they were disabled by the assault guns, and some of them were abandoned by their crews.

The enemy had been forced to give up his intention of defending, both by the fierce attack and by the effective artillery fire, which had caught the enemy motorized column at Ryboly and tank concentrations at Wojszki and in the reserve position in the woods to the southeast, as well as the enemy artillery. While the most advanced enemy riflemen and heavy weapons, supported by tanks, were holding out until the last, everything else was in full flight. Enemy riflemen approximately two companies in strength were observed northwest of Ryboly in scattered retreat (seemingly, the enemy infantry reserve). The enemy artillery left some single guns behind, in their emplacements; the rest withdrew from Ryboly to the northeast and, caught in the pursuit fire of the medium artillery, were abandoned by the enemy north of Ryboly.

Comment:

As in any contemporary account, based on incomplete records, one must allow here for the natural tendency to overestimate the achievement of friendly troops. The Russian strength is nowhere clearly indicated, and it would appear from the account that the German superiority in artillery was decisive, even against Russian tanks. Whatever the final judgement on this small engagement, it remains well worth study as an example of bold and rewarding offensive tactics in a difficult type of operation.

4. THE GERMAN SOLDIER IN DEFENSE

Tactical and Technical Trends, No. 28, July 1st 1943

The following is a translation of an unsigned article which appeared in the semi-official German Army journal Militaer Wochenblatt. The fact that it appears in this normally authoritative and apparently widely read Army journal, and the critical tone in which it is written, show that the conclusions drawn are regarded in army circles as of some importance.

The attack, and only the attack, will make for victory. For this reason our Field Service Regulations rightly state that only offensive conclusion of defensive operations can bring off a decisive victory. But, on the other hand, in the course of any long war, no army is likely to escape defensive operations; no army is strong enough to be attacking everywhere and all the time. Moreover, there are times when it is better to allow the enemy to attack and only go over to the attack yourself when the enemy has thoroughly tied himself up. If the campaigns of 1939, 1940, and early 1941 found the German Army on the defensive only in a very few areas and only for a very short space of time, this was because of the extraordinarily fast tempo of events up to the complete conclusion of the fighting. The importance of defense and its significance in the education and training of troops is not diminished by these facts. In fact, no body of troops knows during its training what tasks it may be called upon to perform. During a war the tactical situations change so quickly, suddenly, and unpredictably that all troops must be educated and trained for defensive as well as for offensive action.

It was quite correct for our military education to lay the chief stress on the attack, as it still does. Moreover, in the past, there was very little time to teach defensive action. But this must not make us fail to recognize, with even more reason, that in concentrated wartime training some subjects are more neglected than others, and in our opinion this applies especially to defense. This article, therefore, will attempt to outline a few points, the teaching of which might well increase the defensive capabilities of the German infantryman, and, moreover, save lives.

The first essential is a sure and ready sense for ground. As is well known, the Higher Command lays down the main battle zone on the map, taking into consideration only major factors, e.g., the siting of artillery, observation posts, and antitank defense, while subordinate commanders subsequently reconnoiter the main defensive line on the ground, taking into consideration, above all, the siting of the infantry support weapons. If junior commanders have time for ground reconnaissance, they will normally find the right position. But if defense is taken up hastily, as is very often the case, then there is a noticeable lack of good judgment. Officers and men, in our opinion, have much too great a tendency to stick to the ground they have first settled on. Judgment of ground in the long run only means, in essentials, getting all the advantages for yourself and giving the enemy all the difficult ground. Naturally, that's easier said than done. But even if, as is usually the case, unfavorable ground has also to be occupied, it is important to recognize this fact and to take the proper tactical measures to make up for it, e.g., siting reserves behind the probable danger area, thickening up antitank defense where the danger from tanks is greatest, etc. Training of this kind can only be carried out on the ground, both with troops and without, by means of a series of very small-scale exercises calling for ground evaluation. In these exercises all units down to the very smallest must be considered in detail. Any high-and-mighty treatment of this subject is out of place. There seems to be by no means the universal recognition that there ought to be, for example, that edges of woods and landmarks, lone trees, etc., are not really suitable for machine-gun positions or observation posts.

The second point where improvement is necessary is camouflage. One has very often the impression that people just haven't grasped the meaning of the word. Camouflage means fitting troops, weapons, equipment, and positions into the landscape. Camouflage that suits one type of ground and one season is nonsense in another type of ground and at another time of year—think of wearing a white snowcoat in the summer. Camouflage is also a matter of time. Positions must be camouflaged before you begin to dig them; observation posts must be camouflaged before you man them; approach roads must be camouflaged or masked before you use them. The basic principle is therefore: camouflage first and dig after, but not vice-versa. People often say: "The enemy isn't firing." Certainly, but he is looking. And as we note down everything we see and plot it on maps giving time and place, and take it to heart, it is clear that the enemy does it just as much. Hence the loss of the most important observation posts at the most critical moment, and the snapping up of runners or reserves on routes which have become known to the enemy. Our troops must have this hammered into them day by day and hour after hour, because such mistakes, though they may not have immediate repercussions, come home to roost sooner or later. In this connection senior officers must set a good example. Well may a brass hat, visiting a front line, expose himself to a little danger to cheer up the troops; in point of fact such conduct seldom draws enemy fire. But if senior officers give away an observation post by their visits, by even so much as one incautious visit, enemy fire is likely to come down later on that observation post and knock it out just when it is needed, which was certainly not the original intention. Don't say that this precaution is exaggerated and unworthy of senior officers. In our opinion everything is wrong which hands it to the enemy on a plate, and everything right which increases defensive capabilities. Our people often lack a sense for little finesses, e.g., use of light and shadow, wariness as regards background. Some time ago we were shown a so-called camouflage suit in use by our enemies, extremely well-made, although to use it ourselves would load our infantry overmuch; but this type of camouflage suit might well be used for training in our reserve battalions. Our people are extremely inventive when they once have something to go on and, having been trained in this way, they might well start making themselves similar suits.

The third essential is a clear recognition of the value of digging.

The German soldier does not like to dig; that is a fact we have to recognize and take measures against in our theoretical and practical training. The Russians are extremely clever in their field fortifications. This dislike of digging comes from the German soldier's innate desire to attack. "We're going forward again soon, what's the point of digging?" Nevertheless our regulations, based on the experience of the last war, emphasize at a number of points the necessity for digging, including during the attack. The regulations say that the troops must so "settle themselves in" in the ground during breathing spaces in the attack that they are exposed as little as possible to enemy fire. In other words: dig in. To say that digging blunts the "edge" of the attack is wrong, because those troops who save their skins in a hole can and will carry forward the attack when the time comes; whereas those who have been killed or wounded in the open are out of it. Hence the prime necessity for convincing junior commanders and troops of the value of digging. But no amount of sticking spades into the ground to "show where the trench should be" will get you there. We must have more, much more, digging. It may cost time and sweat, but it will save lives later. There is no necessity to insist on a regular trench-system in all its ramifications. What is necessary is to teach a man during his training to dig in sufficiently to disappear as soon as possible from the surface in a hole or hollow. We do find in fact that our people recognize this, but unfortunately often only late, after they have had personal experience of men dying because they hadn't dug while men in shallow holes remained alive. A thousand unnecessary fox-holes do less harm than one hole dug too late. Only a cat has more than one life.

The construction of obstacles of all kinds and the laying of wire, etc., should also be very much emphasized. Preparing a village for defense is an art; but we have now learned the proper obstacles to use, and our troops in training should be given the chance to practice with these in a practical manner.

The fourth essential is the recognition of correct behavior, even in quiet periods. We pointed out above what happens to an observation post which is given away, but there are many other instances of this kind. Machine-gun positions are built which stand out like haystacks. They get beautifully camouflaged, but then someone forgets to shut the back, so that the enemy looks straight through them. A CP is set up and becomes the center of footpaths coming in from all sides—which, of course, immediately gives it away. Or you see signs "Look out! Ground covered by enemy!" Now you would think that people would take some notice of this and use the little detour which perhaps takes a quarter of an hour longer.—Nothing of the sort! "The enemy isn't firing and, if he does fire, he won't hit me." This is wrong, of course. Why the sign in the first place, if it isn't? Under this heading also falls the mobile conduct of defense, by which we mean the system of defense in depth introduced after 1916. This means that the main battle zone is a belt in depth. But we have many people who say that the German soldier stays where he has dug himself in. This is naturally correct in so far as it implies that the way through the zone only goes over his dead body. But does this mean that the man has to remain in one spot once the enemy has seen him? Certainly not. In other words, firing positions intended for defense must remain as far as possible unrecognized, which they will only be if no one uses them. We also speak generally of "silent" machine guns. ["Silent" machine guns are set up in the main defensive position out of sight of the enemy and do not participate initially in the combat; they overwhelm the enemy at close range with surprise fire just before he penetrates the position, or after he has already broken into it.] What happens in practice? Our people are too tired to take their machine gun to an alternative position, saying, "They won't spot us—not at once anyway." This is sheer wishful thinking, and leads sooner or later to a catastrophe. The same may be said of observation posts, many artillery positions, CPs, and other military localities. Variety in the siting of outposts, in the routing of patrols and supply convoys is also very much neglected through laziness.

The last point is a purely tactical question. Field Service Regulations speak of a main battle zone whose forward edge is the main line of resistance, i.e., a line which is to be marked out on the ground. But we do hear talk today that the main line of resistance does not suit modern conditions and that positions must be manned by "strongpoints." Apart from the fact that we have not yet seen any official amendment to Field Service Regulations to this effect, we cannot approve this view. Field Service Regulations talk about positions to be sited irregularly and in great depth; it goes on: "At particularly important points, strongpoints containing a number of different types of weapons may be made; neighboring positions must be able to give each other mutual support; eventually, covered communications between all defensive positions must be provided." A difference is obviously made between "positions" and "strongpoints," but only insofar as a "strongpoint" is a "larger position containing a number of different types of weapons." Now if you say that defense is to be "by strongpoints" inasmuch as a number of strongpoints are set up and sited for all-around defense ("hedgehogged off," as the pedants say) and that by reason of this there is no necessity for mutual communication or support, that is a false conclusion. No enemy is going to be so foolish as to attack these so-called strongpoints from the front; he will infiltrate in between them and eventually break in and finally through; these islands of defense, cut off from one another and from any supply from the rear, can and have held for some time, but are sooner or later bound to capitulate unless relieved by a really strong immediate or planned counterattack. But if such strong reserves as those counterattacking were there from the first, one is led to ask why they weren't used from the first in the forward positions. No sensible person lets a burglar inside his house for the purpose of throwing him out again; you make sure from the start that he doesn't get in. In the tactical sense you do that by manning the main battle zone in breadth without any gaps, i.e., by keeping contact to the flanks and also in depth so far as the forces are available, and by giving units regulation frontages.

5. RUSSIAN DEFENSES BEFORE MOSCOW

Tactical and Technical Trends,
No. 26, June 3rd 1943

A brief description of the Russian line of defenses in front of Moscow has been translated from an authoritative German military publication. In the account below, it will be noted that the numbers

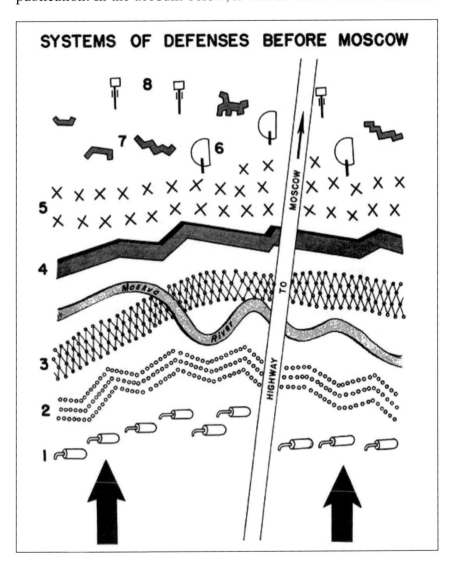

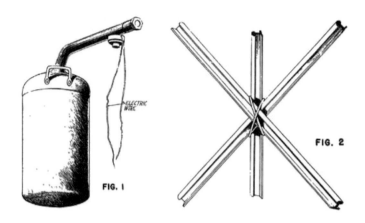

FIG. 1

FIG. 2

refer to defense zones on the sketch map.

Twenty-five miles was the depth of the defense zone which the Soviets had built in front of their capitol to block the way of the German armies. Seven different systems, some very narrow, some in depth, were designed to make the obstacle zone impregnable (see sketch map). At (1) on the map is a long line of flame-throwers (figure 1), of which the tanks were buried in the ground with only the nozzles extending above ground level. On the approach of German soldiers, these devices were to be electrically fired from a hidden bunker.

A deep system of trenches set with upright logs to trap tanks is indicated on the sketch map at 2. The German troops called them "asparagus beds." In addition to the log obstacles, the trenches were heavily mined. Closely adjoining this antitank trench to the rear, along the swampy tributary of the Moskva, was another zone (3), 1 kilometer deep, made up of wire obstacles. Then followed a tank trap (4) in the form of a deep antitank ditch several meters wide. The next defense zone (5) consisted of endless rows of chevaux-de-frise, made of sections of railroad rails welded together (figure 2). Only then were found bunkers (6) of all kinds, and field fortifications (7) as well as artillery emplacements (8).

Comment:

In spite of the elaborate nature of this defense system, the Germans assert that it was successfully penetrated. However, the outcome of the operation indicates that the penetration was limited.

6. GERMAN COMBAT EXPERIENCES IN RUSSIAN WOODED COUNTRY

Tactical and Technical Trends,
No. 26, June 3rd 1943

In many respects, combat in woods is similar to that in towns. Some woods, owing to their location and size, are naturally strong defensive areas. The Germans, it is supposed, derived considerable experience in this kind of warfare during the fighting on the Eastern front. Some of these experiences, based on German sources, are recounted in the following paragraphs.

a. Characteristics

Training for fighting in wooded country not only improves sell-confidence and ability for decisive action, but is at the same time good practice for fighting in darkness and smoke.

The Russians show extraordinary powers of resistance when fighting in marshy and wooded country. They make full use of their exceptional sense of direction and masterly camouflage. They use woods to a large extent, not only for approach, but also in defense, tending, in that latter case, to defend the edges of the wood strongly. The Russian does not give up easily, and therefore the attack in woods must be systematically carried out section by section. The enemy will cover trail crossings with heavy weapons. The difficulty of movement necessitates the allotment of heavy weapons and artillery to units at the start of an operation in order to avoid delays later on.

A coordinated fire plan for attack and defense is often impossible, and reliance must be put on coordinated infantry thrusts. Surprise is a more decisive factor in woods than in open country, and systematic preparation and silence in all movement are essentials.

It is easy in wood fighting to allow one's forces to be split up, especially when patrols, and flank and rear guards, have been detached. Every effort must therefore be made to keep one's forces intact. Movement should be made in deep formations.

A detailed plan must be drawn up, and when a departure from the original plan seems inevitable, permission from the next senior commander must be sought so that he can inform the supporting elements of the changed conditions and avoid any possible danger from one's own fire. (This departs from the modern practice in German tactics, which encourages flexibility of action among junior commanders, and must presumably apply only to the specific conditions of wood fighting).

The results of air reconnaissance are often inadequate, and the employment of numerous and strong fighting patrols is of increasing importance. Efficient signal communication cannot be too strongly stressed.

b. Reconnaissance

Surprise by the enemy must be countered by continual ground reconnaissance. Patrols should be sent to the flanks. Intervals should be sufficiently great (in thick woods, 150 yards) to prevent a patrol from hearing the noise of neighboring patrols, which might often lead to confusion and loss of direction. The arms carried should include submachine guns, rifles (preferably automatic with telescopic sights), and plenty of egg grenades; machine guns are cumbersome. Stick grenades are unsuitable as they easily become lodged in branches. Egg grenades, on the other hand, break their way through. Steel helmets should be left behind; they impair hearing.

- Tasks of patrols must include the following objectives:
- Where is the enemy expected to appear?
- Where is he?
- Where are his flanks?
- How far is he each side of the trails?
- Where is his main line of resistance?
- Which trails and roads does he use?

   Ground reconnaissance must clarify the following:

   Existing roads, trails and clearings, ditches, rivers, and bridges;

Condition of the woods and their undergrowth, such as thickness and height of trees, marshy ground, rises and dips in the ground;

Location of tree snipers.

Trails give valuable information as to the direction the enemy has taken. Branches broken off at about head height, axe marks on tree trunks, and bundles of leaves hanging in branches might be used to show the route taken by the enemy.

c. The March

Under difficult conditions the rate of march is sometimes as low as 2 to 3 miles a day. Engineers must be well forward, and special units for clearing and improving routes must be formed. The help of the local inhabitants as guides must be obtained when possible. Advance guards must be strong enough to envelop enemy forces which are likely to offer resistance along the line of march. Heavy weapons, artillery, headquarters, and signal detachments should also be well forward. Mechanized vehicles with infantry support will be used as protection where possible. Flank and rear guards must be lightly equipped to give them mobility. Antitank weapons and tank-destroying sections must be distributed along the column.

d. Approach

Leave the roads as soon as possible. The thicker the woods, the closer should be the formations. Moves must be made in bounds and covered as far as practicable by heavy weapons and artillery. It has proved worth while to have single rifle squads distributed forward and to the flanks for close-in security. When reaching clearings, trails, etc., and also when leaving woods, a halt should be made to enable patrols to make a careful reconnaissance in order to avoid surprise by ambush and tree snipers. Rifles, submachine guns, and machine guns must not be carried slung, but must be ready for immediate use.

e. Attack

(1) General

In order to effect surprise, feint attacks can often be usefully carried out in woods. Every effort must be made to effect a flanking movement, the enemy being held down frontally by the fire of heavy weapons while strong forces envelop the flanks.

Fire discipline is very important in wood fighting. Irregular, single bursts of rifle and machine-gun fire are of little use. The fire must be controlled in short and heavy bursts. A strong burst of fire has a big moral effect. When the attackers come under fire from the enemy, which will be at quite short range, it has been proved less costly if the attackers rush the intervening ground than if they take up positions and exchange fire. It is no use, after breaking into the enemy's position, to follow up with fire alone, as a withdrawal can easily be made under cover.

The enemy must be speedily reengaged, and given no respite. It must always be remembered that ammunition consumption in wood fighting is heavier than in the open.

(2) Attack against a Weak Opponent

Flanking movement is generally easily accomplished without great loss. Sound signals are best used, as visual signals are readily missed.

(3) Attack against a Strong Opponent

Assault troops armed with close combat weapons and supported by flamethrowers must break into the enemy's position and effect a narrow penetration. It will often pay to make a surprise breakthrough without first opening fire. Heavy mortars and single light infantry and antitank guns will generally be allotted to the rifle companies. Antitank shells can be used very effectively in woods. Numerous observers must be placed well forward to direct the artillery.

f. Clearing a Wood

Combing through woods over a wide area with intervals of a few yards between each man has been proved ineffectual, because there is always the risk that the enemy having concentrated his forces can easily break through the weak line. The rule must be to keep one's forces together and send in strong assault support from various directions with the aim of encircling the enemy. This must be the subject of very careful and coordinated planning on a time basis. Attempts to break out of the wood must be countered by covering the edges with fire from heavy weapons and artillery, as well as by the employment of tanks and assault guns.

g. Defense

To avoid being surprised there must be constant reconnaissance; it is wrong to wait for the enemy to approach under cover; it is right to search him out and destroy him wherever he is. The very mobility of the defense deceives the enemy as to one's strength and intentions. Reserves must be ready to make counterattacks. Woods offer numerous possibilities for obstacles in depth; these hold up the enemy or divert him to routes favoring defensive fire. If time is too short for construction of continuous defensive positions, every effort must be made to arrange strongpoints of resistance, with all-around defense if possible. These should be surrounded by mines. Weapons should be placed 30 to 50 yards behind the edge of the woods, so long as visibility is not impaired. Wood defense requires a large number of observation posts, and signal equipment must be obtained from the division signal unit for the necessary links. Trails must be cleared of dry wood and other material which causes noise. Wire must be anchored to the ground; otherwise, its removal with implements such as hay-forks is possible. Listening posts must be changed daily.

h. Training

The following points in training are particularly important:

(1) Individual

Silent movement; working forward in thick undergrowth; crawling in various types of woods; visual training and indication of targets; finding direction; marking routes, and recognition of enemy markings of routes; cover and camouflage; close combat and engaging tree snipers; antitank close combat in woods; tree observers; patrols; pickets; firing in woods.

(2) Heavy Weapons

Transporting heavy weapons; rapid emplacement; creating fields of fire; observation and keeping contact; reporting targets; fire coordination.

(3) Engineers

Building bridges and dams, and clearing paths and trails in marshy ground; rapid removal of tree obstacles in depth; building wire and tree obstacles; building observation posts; preparing gun positions and making clearances in the field of fire.

(4) Formations

Formations for movement and fighting in woods; marching to the sides of trails and by night; movement by bounds; quick deployment; surprise with light and heavy weapons; attack on limited objectives; coming under enemy fire; break into enemy position, and quick exploitation of success; defense alarms; reserves counterattack; security at night.

7. NOTES ON GERMAN ARMORED UNITS

Tactical and Technical Trends, No. 24, May 6th 1943

The following pages contain an edited translation of training notes on some of the tactical courses given at the Panzer Troop School (School of Mobile Troops, at Wünsdorf, Germany). Though dealing specifically with armored units, this material should be of interest to all branches of the service.

The types of German tanks mentioned below are the PzKw 2, 3, and 4. The PzKw 2 is a 10-ton tank capable of about 35 mph, usually equipped with one 20-mm gun and a machine gun. The PzKw 3 is a 19-ton tank with heavier armor, and with a speed of about 28 mph; it is usually equipped with a 50-mm gun and 2 machine guns. The PzKw 4, with still thicker armor plate, weighs 21 to 22 tons, and has one 75-mm gun and 2 machine guns; its top speed is 22 mph.

I CLOSE RECONNAISSANCE BY A TANK REGIMENT

a. General

(1) Close reconnaissance by the tank regiment will be carried out for the benefit of the regiment only.

(2) For this mission the following units are available:

The PzKw 2s of the light tank platoons in the regimental and battalion headquarters companies. *[Regimental and battalion headquarters companies include a light tank platoon equipped with PzKw 2s.]*

The motorcycle reconnaissance platoons of the headquarters companies.

Moreover, all crews of light and medium tanks must be qualified to carry out close reconnaissance when conditions permit *[Probably has reference to tanks in the tank companies. In this connection it should be noted that the light PzKw 2 is no longer included in the tank company. The light tank company is now equipped only with PzKw 3s, and the medium tank company with PzKw 4s.]*

(3) The PzKw 2 tank is entirely suitable for cross-country work. On account of its stronger armor it is superior to the armored reconnaissance car, although this car carries a gun of larger caliber. According to the situation, the tank is expected to defeat a numerically stronger but unarmored enemy who is not prepared for defense.

As the enemy may well suspect the presence of a tank unit if one or more tanks are sighted, battle or tactical reconnaissance by tanks is not permitted when an armored attack is contemplated against an enemy with well-prepared defenses and a high morale. In this situation, the reconnaissance is carried out by motorcycle platoons. For this reason, in many cases squads of the motorcycle reconnaissance platoons in battalion headquarters companies form a valuable supplement to the light tank platoon—for example, with motorcycle reconnaissance elements in front of a point of light tanks.

(4) The light tank platoons are equipped with radio transmitters and receivers, but the range is short. If the ground to be reconnoitered is beyond the radio range, motorcycle messengers must be added or relay radio stations established.

b. Orders for Reconnaissance

(1) Close reconnaissance is ordered by the regimental commander as a matter of routine. He directs the assembling of the patrol.

(2) Orders for the patrol should include:

- Information concerning the enemy, as known to the officer issuing the order;
- Plan of operation, including the time phases during the reconnaissance;
- Mission for the patrol, together with the route and measures to be taken in case of road blocks, mines, and enemy contact:
- The missions, routes, and reconnaissance limits of other patrols;
- Duration of the reconnaissance;

- Means of communication;
- Where to rejoin the command;
- Where messages may reach the commanding officer.

(3) Composition of Patrols

As a general rule, patrols will be formed from motorcycle reconnaissance squads of the headquarters companies. They are trained to cooperate properly. These patrols must be especially strong if contact with the enemy is expected and it is necessary to fight for information.

While the regiment is on the march, at rest periods, during alerts, and after the objective has been reached, parts of the motorcycle platoons and of the light tank platoons will be used for security missions.

When attacking an enemy whose strength is uncertain, or after a successful break-through, the light tank platoons of the leading battalions will be employed as patrols.

II NOTES ON MISSIONS AND OPERATIONS OF TANK PLATOONS

Although brief, the following outline suggests main points covered in the tactical training of German tank platoons, particularly with regard to the character of missions assigned to these units. The original notes were accompanied by references, omitted here, to German training documents and manuals.

a. Combat Platoons

(1) Ordinary Operations
- Point platoon (alone or in cooperation with motorcycle reconnaissance platoon).
- Attack against heavy infantry weapons.
- Attack against artillery.
- Attack against infantry:
- While the platoon is in motion;
- From a prepared position.
- Close support of friendly infantry:
- After the second wave, or echelon, of tanks has passed friendly

riflemen;
- Riflemen of armored units.
- Fighting for an important terrain feature.
- Battle against enemy tanks:
- Evenly matched;
- Against heavy odds;
- Unexpected encounters;
- Enemy tanks surprising our own;
- Our own tanks surprising enemy tanks.
- Advancing during attack, but behind our own front line.
- Conduct of an armored unit which has reached its objective.
- Transition from attack to defense.
- Defense against close-in attack.

(2) Special Operations
- Attack against permanent fortifications.
- Attack against a river line.
- Attack against villages and wooded areas.
- Combat at night or in fog.
- Procedure on encountering mines.

b. Light Tank Platoon *[Part of regimental and battalion headquarters companies; platoon is equipped with PzKw 2s]*
(1) The Individual Tank
- When attacking an insufficiently reconnoitered enemy.
- After breaking through the enemy infantry zone.
- After reaching the objective.
- Security in bivouac, or in prepared positions subject to attack.

(2) The Unit
- Unit as point, or flank guard.
- Reconnaissance for determining terrain and enemy position, as the basis for the beginning of an armored attack.
- After a successful penetration of the enemy infantry zone, determination of hostile dispositions and nature of the terrain to the front and flanks.
- After reaching its objective.
- Reconnaissance to determine the enemy's position during the

counterattack.

- The unit, reinforced with engineers, to make surprise attack to capture a bridge, blow up railroads or bridges, or lay mine obstacles.

III ORDER OF MARCH OF A TANK BATTALION OF THREE COMPANIES AS ADVANCED GUARD

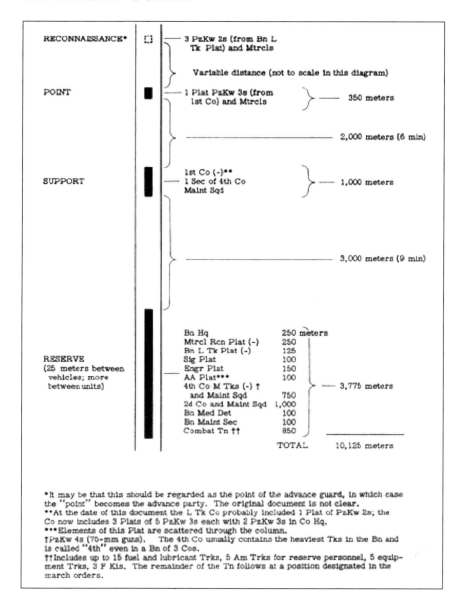

RECONNAISSANCE*   [:]   —— 3 PzKw 2s (from Bn L Tk Plat) and Mtrcls

Variable distance (not to scale in this diagram)

POINT   ■   — 1 Plat PzKw 3s (from 1st Co) and Mtrcls   —— 350 meters

———————————— 2,000 meters (6 min)

SUPPORT   ▌   — 1st Co (-)** / 1 Sec of 4th Co Maint Sqd   —— 1,000 meters

———————————— 3,000 meters (9 min)

RESERVE (25 meters between vehicles; more between units)	Bn Hq	250 meters
	Mtrcl Rcn Plat (-)	250
	Bn L Tk Plat (-)	125
	Sig Plat	100
	Engr Plat	150
	AA Plat***	100
	4th Co M Tks (-) † and Maint Sqd	750
	2d Co and Maint Sqd	1,000
	Bn Med Det	100
	Bn Maint Sec	100
	Combat Tn ††	850

—— 3,775 meters

TOTAL   10,125 meters

*It may be that this should be regarded as the point of the advance guard, in which case the "point" becomes the advance party. The original document is not clear.
**At the date of this document the L Tk Co probably included 1 Plat of PzKw 2s; the Co now includes 3 Plats of 5 PzKw 3s each with 2 PzKw 3s in Co Hq.
***Elements of this Plat are scattered through the column.
†PzKw 4s (75-mm guns). The 4th Co usually contains the heaviest Tks in the Bn and is called "4th" even in a Bn of 3 Cos.
††Includes up to 15 fuel and lubricant Trks, 5 Am Trks for reserve personnel, 5 equipment Trks, 3 F Kis. The remainder of the Tn follows at a position designated in the march orders.

IV ORDER OF MARCH OF A REINFORCED ARMORED INFANTRY BATTALION

(Acting as Advance Guard; Speed, 20 mph)

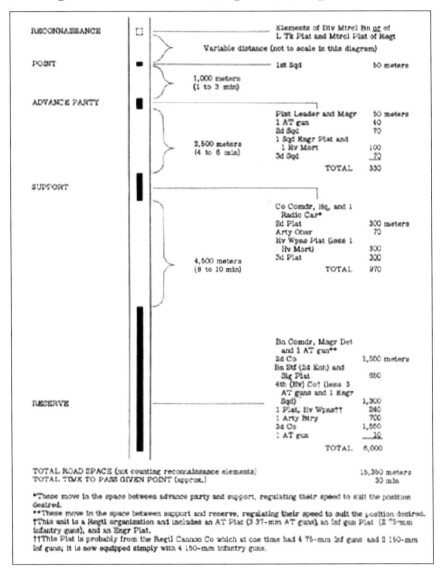

RECONNAISSANCE		Elements of Div Mtrcl Bn or of L Tk Plat and Mtrcl Plat of Regt	
		Variable distance (not to scale in this diagram)	
POINT		1st Sqd	50 meters
	1,000 meters (1 to 3 min)		
ADVANCE PARTY		Plat Leader and Magr	50 meters
		1 AT gun	40
		2d Sqd	70
	2,500 meters (4 to 6 min)	1 Sqd Engr Plat and 1 Hv Mort	100
		3d Sqd	70
		TOTAL	330
SUPPORT		Co Comdr, Hq, and 1 Radio Car*	
		2d Plat	300 meters
		Arty Obsr	70
		Hv Wpns Plat (less 1 Hv Mort)	300
	4,500 meters (8 to 10 min)	3d Plat	300
		TOTAL	970
RESERVE		Bn Comdr, Magr Det and 1 AT gun**	
		2d Co	1,500 meters
		Bn Stf (2d Ech) and Sig Plat	650
		4th (Hv) Co† (less 3 AT guns and 1 Engr Sqd)	1,300
		1 Plat, Hv Wpns††	340
		1 Arty Btry	700
		3d Co	1,500
		1 AT gun	10
		TOTAL	6,000

TOTAL ROAD SPACE (not counting reconnaissance elements) 15,360 meters
TOTAL TIME TO PASS GIVEN POINT (approx.) 30 min

*These move in the space between advance party and support, regulating their speed to suit the position desired.
**These move in the space between support and reserve, regulating their speed to suit the position desired.
†This unit is a Regtl organization and includes an AT Plat (3 37-mm AT guns), an Inf gun Plat (2 75-mm infantry guns), and an Engr Plat.
††This Plat is probably from the Regtl Cannon Co which at one time had 4 75-mm Inf guns and 2 150-mm Inf guns; it is now equipped simply with 4 150-mm infantry guns.

V NOTES ON MARCH DISCIPLINE OF MOTORIZED TROOPS

a. The Fundamental Principles for the March of Smaller Units

(1) Mounting up, Starting, and Halting

Everyone will sit quietly after mounting the vehicles. At the signal or command "Forward," the vehicles will be set in motion. If possible, all vehicles should begin to move at the same time. Vehicles which fail to move off with the others cause confusion. Therefore, a preparatory signal should be given. As they move out, all vehicles will follow the leading vehicle at the designated distance. The minimum distance should be 20 meters. During halts, distances are in no case to be less than 20 meters. This distance may be shortened to 5 or even 2 meters when the tactical or traffic situation so demands.

Besides the driver, all vehicles will have assigned to them leaders who are responsible for the transmission of signals. The following signals will be used: "Slow down;" "Turn to right;" "Halt;" "Turn sharply to right;" "Take cover from air raid;" "Turn left." Personnel are always to dismount on the right-hand side. Crossings, curves, etc. are to be left clear. Traffic control personnel are to be posted along the line of march.

(2) Distances

Distances are to be not less than 20 meters. If the distance is too great, vehicles are to proceed at gradually increased speed to close the gap, rather than racing ahead. Platoon leaders must keep control of their units. The observance of the regulation distances is not to be rigidly insisted upon; the type of vehicle, route, and terrain are to be considered. Distances of 50 to 150 meters are to be maintained between units (i.e., companies, etc.). The signals, "Take more distance" or "Close up" should be given only in exceptional cases. The basic principle is to give as few signals as possible; otherwise march discipline will become lax and drivers will pay no heed to the signals.

(3) Speed

This depends on the condition of the road, and on the terrain, weather, and type of vehicles. Average speed is not to be insisted upon; however, the speed of the leading vehicle should be set by order. The following table may serve as a guide in fixing the speed of the leading vehicle:

For units with a preponderance of:

	DAY	NIGHT
Full-track vehicles	20 km ph (12 1/2 mph)	12 km ph (7 1/2 mph)
Half-track vehicles	30 km ph (18 1/2 mph)	15 km ph (9 1/2 mph)
Four-wheeled vehicles	35 km ph (22 mph)	18 km ph (11 mph)
Motorcycles	40 km ph (25 mph)	20 km ph (12 1/2 mph)

Vehicles move off at a slow speed, which is then gradually increased when the whole unit is in motion. Speed is not to be increased or decreased too suddenly. Even very brief halts in front will unfavorably affect the rest of the column.

(4) Passing

The overtaken vehicle must pull over to the right and give the "go ahead" signal, and must not increase its speed. Columns may be doubled without special permission by: single vehicles with officers, personnel moving forward to receive orders, messengers, medical and veterinary officers, supply sergeants, signal personnel, and staff personnel with appropriate command flags. Marching columns must not be overtaken by another column. Stationary or slowly moving columns may be doubled only if their commanders are consulted first, or if an order to this effect issued by a higher authority is produced. A halted column must not be put in motion while it is being passed.

(5) Turning

To turn around, individual vehicles will veer sharply to the right and then turn. The lead vehicle again takes position at the head and the units follow in the old order, or in the order in which they find themselves after making the turn.

(6) The Last Vehicle and Dropping Out

The rear of every unit is brought up by a vehicle carrying an officer or a senior NCO. He decides whether or not vehicles which have dropped out should remain behind, and he reports his decision to the unit commander. He prevents unauthorized passing of the column by other columns when it is halted. The last vehicle must display a red-and-white light at night. Vehicles which have dropped out will get off the road, hoist the "drop-out" flag, and motion other vehicles to pass. Maintenance sections will repair minor defects, or order the drivers to do so. When these have been repaired, vehicles must not double other columns to catch up, but must attach themselves to the nearest unit and then proceed to their own units at the next scheduled halt.

(7) Night Marches

Vehicles using their parking lights will proceed at moderate speed. Under certain circumstances distances are to be decreased and the units separated. Careful route reconnaissance and traffic posts are essential. Signals are to be given with the flashlight. The same principles apply in case of fog.

b. Basic Principles for the March of Larger Units

(1) Preparations

Advance route reconnaissance should be initiated. The condition and width of roads, bridges, cover, etc., are to be reconnoitered. The effects of sudden freezing or rain should be considered. All personnel, and the drivers in particular, must be well acquainted with the route and destination. The march order must include: the route, destination, order of march, place and hour of assembly for the march, halts and rests, reconnaissance, security measures, regulation of traffic, and administrative details.

(2) Assembling the Initial Point

A timetable is to be drawn up. An initial point must be designated outside the bivouac area, but in the direction of the march. Before the column is assembled a representative from each unit must contact the liaison officer of the unit that is to precede it. The crossing of columns is to be avoided. Lining up without confusion is to be demanded. A short halt is to be made at the initial point. Jamming at the initial point is to be avoided. If possible, there should be no assembling and halting on the road or route to the initial point.

(3) The March

Long columns will be split up into a number of march groups. These travel with considerable distance between groups. These distances must not be shortened by vehicles from the rear groups closing on the group in the front. Any differences in distances due to varying rate of speed are to be adjusted at the next halt. It is the duty of every officer to take energetic measures in case of traffic jams.

(4) Halts

Twenty-minute halts should be ordered every two hours. As a rule they take place on the road. Vehicles should park on the extreme right of the road and cover should be sought. The vehicles are to be inspected. Special halts for maintenance purposes will not be provided for.

(5) Rests

Rests should be ordered every 4 or 5 hours and should be of at least 2 and 1/2 hours' duration. Time and space should be considered when ordering rest periods. If the march is properly regulated as to time, everyone will be able to adhere to the time schedule and get off the road to take cover. During rests an officer collects messages from every company for the information of the column commander on the condition of vehicles, oil and fuel supply, etc. During the rest, the fuel tanks are refilled, minor repairs undertaken, and the troops fed. Roads should be cleared for the resumption of the march.

(6) Traffic Regulation

Each unit is responsible for the regulation of its own traffic. Motorcycle messengers, squads, or even whole platoons may be assigned to regulate traffic. In case of large units, the higher echelons may establish traffic control. The regulations issued by higher echelons must be strictly adhered to. The responsibility for the regulation of traffic must be definitely assigned by order.

8. TACTICS OF STREET FIGHTING ON THE RUSSIAN FRONT

Tactical and Technical Trends,
No. 26, June 3rd 1943

In the Battle of France street fighting played but a small part, since at no time were the Germans forced to assault an important town or city against prepared and determined resistance. Operations in North Africa have not involved street fighting on an appreciable scale. However, the story is different on the Eastern Front. The fact is that this type of fighting has been one of the significant features of operations on the Russian front since the winter of 1941-42, and it may well prove of major importance in possible future operations in Western Europe with its many cities and towns.

With a few exceptions, such as the defense of Sevastopol and Stalingrad, the importance of street fighting in centers of population on the Russian front appears to have been largely overlooked. The following British report on street fighting on this front is therefore of interest. This report is felt to be reliable and to present a good analysis of the tactical principles involved.

a. Strategic Importance of Town Defense in Russia

Fighting for, and inside, towns and villages on the Eastern Front has developed to a point where it has become of primary strategic importance in certain phases of the campaign.

(1) Early Period: Failure to Defend Towns

During the summer and autumn campaigns of 1941, fighting inside towns and villages did not play an important role in operations. Although the Russians did put up strong resistance in and around certain key towns, like Minsk and Smolensk, on the whole the German strategy of deep and rapid encirclement forced the Russians to abandon valuable towns in an attempt to extricate their armies. Certain cities were defended with great determination, namely, Odessa, Leningrad, and Moscow—but in each case all the fighting took place at their approaches.

(2) Later Period: Towns Are Defended

(a) First Phase: German Defense of Towns

The first phase of the campaign in which street fighting became important was during the Russian offensive in the winter of 1941-42, when the Germans stemmed the Russian advance by their determined defense of key towns and villages along the whole front. The tactical setting for this period of fighting was largely determined by the peculiar climatic conditions, in that an exceptionally cold winter and double the normal depth of snow denied ±o the Russians all freedom of maneuver and imposed on their troops a tremendous degree of hardship. The Germans were able to keep relatively warm in centers of population and to concentrate on the defense of the main approaches, and resorted to stubborn and costly street fighting whenever the Russians did manage to break into a town or village.

(b) Second Phase: Russian Defense of Towns

The second phase of important street fighting was during the latter period of the Russian retreat in the summer and autumn of 1942 in southern Russia and Caucasia. Throughout July and in August, the Germans had advanced rapidly and had overwhelmed Russian resistance in some sectors by local air and tank supremacy. The Russians, at first, attempted to stop the Germans by getting off the main routes of German advance and striking at their lines of communication and supply, but this only interfered with enemy progress and did not stem his advance.

The Soviet High Command then issued strict orders that all withdrawals were to stop and every town and village must be defended street by street and house by house whether it was surrounded or not. This policy was put into effect with determination and ruthlessness, and achieved virtual stabilization of the whole front toward the end of August and throughout September, October, and November. This, in spite of the fact that in the steppe-type of country in southern Russia and north Caucasia the Germans had every facility to maneuver around centers of population. However, the determined defense in depth of all key points on main lines of communication made a sustained offensive by the enemy extremely difficult. The Russians were told to fight in towns even partially destroyed by aerial bombardment, and were taught to appreciate the tactical advantage of fighting in ruins.

(c) Third Phase: Stalingrad

The third phase in the development of the tactics of street fighting centers around the Russian defense of the city of Stalingrad; this operation was of the utmost significance to the whole course of the campaign on the Eastern Front and raised the tactics of street fighting to a level of importance never before envisaged. In this case, determined street fighting inside a large and unfortified city enabled the Russians to deny to the enemy one of the principal strategic goals of his summer campaign—the cutting of Russian communications along the Volga River.

b. First Phase—January - April 1942

(1) German System of Defense

Invariably the Germans prepare a town or village, likely to be attacked, for all-around defense. There is usually a belt of field fortifications outside the populated center, with ditches, minefields and other antitank obstacles protecting all approaches, every obstacle being covered by fire according to a well coordinated fire plan. Antitank weapons and obstacles are generally concentrated along the main avenues of probable tank approach, usually in the outskirts of the town or village.

The populated center itself is fortified according to a carefully designed plan, with emphasis laid on the importance of the element of surprise in all street fighting. Certain buildings are transformed into fortified strongholds, and several such buildings, capable of mutual fire support, form a defense area. Streets and houses which are outside these zones are covered by small-arms fire.

The ground floor of the fortified point is usually reserved for heavy weapons: artillery guns, antitank guns, and mortars. Sometimes tanks are placed in ambush inside barns or buildings, or partly dug in along the outskirts of the town where they might be least expected and,

49

generally, covering the approaches to a fortified zone.

Heavy and light automatic weapons, snipers, and grenade-throwers are dispersed on the upper floors and on roof tops.

Artillery and mortars are also emplaced in parks, gardens, and courtyards and are more effective in repelling tanks than in close fighting.

If one or two buildings of a fortified zone are lost, the Germans attempt to counterattack vigorously before the enemy has time to consolidate his position.

(2) Russian Methods of Attack

(a) Preparation

Through costly experience the Russians learned that it is "the surprise nature of enemy fire in street fighting that has the deadliest effect," and that it is "often more difficult to find out where the enemy strongpoints are than it is to reduce them after they have been discovered"

Hence, the first prerequisite of a successful attack on a town or village according to Russian teaching is to determine the plan of enemy defense in detail, and to prepare a coordinated plan of attack, also in meticulous detail.

Therefore, the Russians insist on the value of detailed intelligence, which must aim not only at locating the fortified zones in the town, but also determining the defensive fire plan and locating the principal weapons. The importance of discovering means of approach to the fortified zones which will afford the best cover is equally stressed.

If all this cannot be established from intelligence sources, thorough reconnaissance and even reconnaissance in force to draw enemy fire is recommended. A detailed plan of the town or village is drawn, if one does not exist, and the probable enemy system of defense is sketched in. Then the plan of attack is worked out in detail.

(b) The Attack

(1) The Approach

The Russians stress the importance of surprise. If reconnaissance has been thorough or local guides are available, they prefer to attack by night. If possible, the attack is carried out by simultaneous thrusts from different directions. A feint is made generally to pin down the main antitank weapons. Although the objective may be surrounded prior to the attack, an avenue of retreat is left to the enemy, for experience has taught that cornered Germans fight desperately and that reducing fortified buildings is more expensive in casualties than is fighting in the open. Therefore, the attempt is made to force the enemy to retreat after a number of strongholds are taken and after the probable line of retreat is ambushed.

The Russians usually employed tanks in attacking villages, but used them sparingly, and often to pin down the main defensive weapons rather than to rush the defenses and take part in street fighting. Often the tanks are thrown in from an entirely different direction from the main infantry attack, but the importance of coordinating and timing these various blows is always stressed.

Close artillery and mortar support is insisted upon. A preliminary bombardment or creeping barrage to cover the approach is not usually necessary. The main thing is to plan and coordinate artillery and heavy mortar fire with the action of other arms and, in the initial stages, attempt to distract or deceive the enemy in order to effect the maximum surprise.

(2) Fighting to Reduce Strongholds

For fighting inside villages and towns the Russians rely principally on infantrymen armed with submachine guns, hand grenades, and bottles containing an incendiary mixture. Although the importance of training all infantry units in the art of street fighting is continually stressed, it is considered advisable to train and equip special detachments of assault troops for this task. It is not known how these groups are organized and whether each infantry battalion, regiment, or division has such detachments. It is known that each detachment is subdivided into a reconnaissance force and a main body. The reconnaissance detachment ascertains the best lines of approach and the cover which will enable the assaulting forces to approach their objective. The main body specializes in assault tactics and in hand-to-hand fighting.

The assault troops are taught to avoid advancing along streets or across squares. They must find their way to their objective by using back yards, fences, and lanes, and even by making their way from house to house, breaking through walls or moving from roof to roof if necessary.

The objective of an assault group should be to isolate and reduce a group of fortified buildings which compose a stronghold, and then go on to the next objective if necessary.

The importance of effective artillery support is stressed, but the difficulty of providing it is fully realized. The following procedure is recommended. Before the attack the infantry and artillery commander agree on a preliminary, definite, and simple plan of artillery support and establish a number of Very light signals, preferably, to indicate the progress of the attack.

On the other hand, it is the duty of artillery and mortar commanders to keep in the closest possible touch with the assaulting troops and to use their initiative in giving them close support wherever circumstances permit. A proportion of guns is actually moved forward to take on targets over open sights and to take part in street fighting.

(3) Consolidation to Repel Counterattacks

The Russians have learned from experience that the German is a skillful and dangerous opponent as long as he can keep his enemy at a distance by effective fire, but that he dislikes hand-to-hand fighting. Thus if the ground floor of a building is captured, there is usually no difficulty in clearing the rest of the house, but if a strongpoint is lost and the Germans have been forced to withdraw by hand-to-hand fighting, they usually stage an immediate and determined counterattack from a new direction.

Hence the importance is stressed of mopping up the ground taken, clearing it of booby traps and mines, and fortifying it against counterattacks as quickly as possible.

It is usual to assign the mission of fortifying and garrisoning a captured stronghold to a specially trained group forming part of the assault detachment.

c. Second Phase—August - November 1942

(1) German Method of Attack

The German methods of attack on towns and villages along their line of advance in southern Russian and Caucasia were radically different from the Russian methods under conditions of winter warfare.

Whenever the Germans expected to meet Russian resistance at a key point, they preferred to disorganize the defense by terrific aerial bombardment and rushing the defenses in their stride by a massed tank attack. Their local air supremacy and speed of advance, and the lack of natural obstacles, contributed to the surprise of such an onslaught.

(2) Russian System of Defense

The Russians gradually developed the following means of combating the German blitz tactics:

(a) To prevent the enemy from rushing the town defenses with tanks, a belt of defensive works was constructed in length outside the town. The depth and intricacy of these defenses depended on the garrison available for their defense.

(b) Inside the town, houses are reinforced and organized for defense in groups, as on the German pattern, with artillery emplaced on ground floors, in barns, squares, and parks.

(c) Particular attention is paid to antitank defenses. The Russians insist that tank obstacles to be effective must be planned with ingenuity and cunning. An ordinary tank barrier covered by fire is of little effect. The object should be to erect tank obstacles and traps so as to force the tanks to hesitate or turn and be taken by surprise. For instance, if along the probable avenue of tank approach obstacles are erected in the form of a labyrinth which would force the tanks to maneuver around and through the obstacles, this would allow the garrison to deal with the tanks effectively both by well-concealed antitank guns and rifles and by bundles of hand grenades and incendiary bottles.

(d) The principal lesson which the Russian Command had to teach their troops was that a town or village largely burnt down or even destroyed by preliminary air attacks, was even more suited to prolonged and stubborn defense than one with all its buildings intact.

The troops are taught to improvise fortified nests among ruins and charred remains of houses as quickly as possible, and to provide a number of alternative sites, all interconnected by a system of deep trenches. The debris offers greater opportunities for camouflage, surprise, and ambush than do standing buildings, is not as likely to be affected by subsequent bombardment, and is not vulnerable to incendiary attack.

(e) After the enemy has penetrated the area of the town or village, the importance of surprise counterattacks, when and where he least expects them, is stressed. In order to achieve this, it is important not to give away one's position or fire plan by movement or desultory firing; hence, practically all essential movement is restricted to the night. It is then that supplies and ammunition are brought up and the wounded evacuated.

(f) In preparing fortified positions the importance of eliminating all dead space is stressed. This can be best achieved by enfilading fire and by having mobile groups armed with submachine guns make use of available or improvised cover to attack enemy assault groups in flank and rear. The Russians make excellent use of snipers whose special task is to pick off officers and NCO's. The Germans have suffered heavy casualties among artillery forward observers, who keep in the vanguard of the assault to control the supporting artillery fire more effectively.

(g) It is never advisable to erect tank obstacles or barricades in front of firing points, because the enemy expects it and it is only likely to draw his fire.

d. Third Phase—Defense of Stalingrad

Street fighting tactics in the fighting at Stalingrad (August 26 - November 23) were on the whole no different from those outlined for phase two—both with regard to the methods of German attack or Russian defense—but the scope, intensity, and versatility of these tactics have not been paralleled in this war.

Before even reaching the city's outer defenses, which had been improvised apparently in haste and probably consisted of ordinary field defenses, the Germans pulverized Stalingrad by continuous aerial bombardment. Then followed repeated assaults supported by great numbers of tanks. This is how a German officer described these first assaults on Stalingrad:

"The attacking German troops move forward behind tanks and assault guns, sweep away barricades with gun fire, knock holes into house-walls, and crush down wire obstacles. Guns and mortars batter concealed positions, antitank guns cover the side streets against possible flanking operations by tanks, antiaircraft guns are ready to meet attacking aircraft. Low-flying aircraft and Stukas attack the rear sections of resistance in the inner town, and the supply points and routes inside the town. Machine guns engage snipers on the roofs. Covered thus, infantry and engineer assault detachments, keeping close to the walls, advance over the wreckage from street to street, break down blocked doors and cellar windows with explosive charges and grenades, smoke out the less accessible corners with flame-throwers, and comb houses from ground floor to roof. In all this, they have frequently to engage the enemy in hand-to-hand fighting."

These assaults failed to make much progress, partly due to the great quantity of artillery concentrated by the Russians, and partly due to the way in which the large number of reinforced concrete and stone buildings were adapted by the Russians for defense, even when they were in a ruined condition.

The Germans were virtually forced to give up large-scale tank attacks as being too costly, and the fighting reverted to intense street fighting between relatively small infantry and engineer assault groups, liberally supplied with flamethrowers.

The main difference between the fighting in Stalingrad and that which took place at other inhabited localities along the Eastern Front was that considerable quantities of artillery of every caliber participated on both sides. Many of the Russian batteries were emplaced on the islands and the east bank of the Volga, while others remained among the ruins of the town. The whole site of the city became a complicated tangle of trenches, deep dugouts under blasted buildings, and strongholds in ruins or in the remains of large and strong reinforced concrete buildings, such as abounded in the vast factory area. Here, the theory that the ruins of a city constitute one of the most formidable types of fortification in modern war, was proved to the hilt.

9. RUSSIAN TANK TACTICS AGAINST GERMAN TANKS

Tactical and Technical Trends,
No. 16, January 14th 1943

The following report is a literal translation of a portion of a Russian publication concerning the most effective methods of fire against German tanks.

For the successful conduct of fire against enemy tanks, we should proceed as follows:

a. Manner of Conducting Fire for the Destruction of Enemy Tanks

(1) While conducting fire against enemy tanks, and while maneuvering on the battlefield, our tanks should seek cover in partially defiladed positions.

(2) In order to decrease the angle of impact of enemy shells, thereby decreasing their power of penetration, we should try to place our tanks at an angle to the enemy.

(3) In conducting fire against German tanks, we should carefully observe the results of hits, and continue to fire until we see definite signs of a hit (burning tanks, crew leaving the tank, shattering of the tank or the turret). Watch constantly enemy tanks which do not show these signs, even though they show no signs of life. While firing at the active tanks of the enemy, one should be in full readiness to renew the battle against those apparently knocked out.

b. Basic Types of German Tanks and their Most Vulnerable Parts

The types of tanks most extensively used in the German Army are the following: the 11-ton Czech tank, the Mark III, and the Mark IV. The German self-propelled assault gun (Sturmgeschütz) has also been extensively used.

In addition to the above-mentioned types of tanks, the German Army uses tanks of all the occupied countries; in their general tactical and technical characteristics, their armament and armor, these tanks are inferior.

(1) Against the 11-ton Czech tank, fire as follows:

(a) From the front—against the turret and gun-shield, and below the turret gear case;

(b) From the side—at the third and fourth bogies, against the driving sprocket, and at the gear case under the turret;

(c) From behind—against the circular opening and against the exhaust vent.

Remarks: In frontal fire, with armor-piercing shells, the armor of the turret may be destroyed more quickly than the front part of the hull. In firing at the side and rear, the plates of the hull are penetrated more readily than the plates of the turret.

(2) Against Mark III tanks, fire as follows:

(a) From the front—at the gun mantlet and at the driver's port, and the machine-gun mounting;

(b) From the side—against the armor protecting the engine, and against the turret ports;

(c) From behind—directly beneath the turret, and at the exhaust vent.

Remarks: In firing from the front against the Mark III tank, the turret is more vulnerable than the front of the hull and the turret gear box. In firing from behind, the turret is also more vulnerable than the rear of the hull.

(3) Against the self-propelled assault gun, fire as follows:

(a) From the front—against the front of the hull, the drivers port, and below the tube of the gun;

(b) From the side—against the armor protecting the engine, and the turret.

(c) From behind—against the exhaust vent and directly beneath the turret.

(4) Against the Mark IV, fire as follows:

(a) From the front—against the turret, under the tube of the gun, against the driver's port, and the machine-gun mounting;

(b) From the side—at the center of the hull at the engine compartment, and against the turret port.

(c) From behind—against the turret, and against the exhaust vent.

Remarks: It should be noted that in firing against the front of this tank, the armor of the turret is more vulnerable than the front plate of the turret gear box, and of the hull. In firing at the sides of the tank, the armor plate of the engine compartment and of the turret, is more vulnerable than the armor of the turret gear box.

10. A GERMAN SPEARHEAD IN THE KIEV OPERATION

Illustrierte Beobachter, October 16th, 23rd, 30th, November 6th and 13th, 1941

THE ADVANCE OF THE SIXTH ARMY
GENERAL VON REICHENAU'S ARMY.

Among the German forces which crossed the Russian frontier on June 22, 1941, was the Sixth Army, under the command of Field Marshal General von Reichenau. It appears that this army, on the eve of the campaign, was concentrated in German-held Poland in the Biala-Chelm sector immediately west of the Bug River (the Russo-German boundary under the agreement of August 21, 1939). The Sixth Army held the northern flank of the German South Group of Armies under Field Marshal General von Rundstedt. The Sixth Army included motorized infantry and panzer divisions, the Adolph Hitler Regiment (an S.S. unit), and foot infantry divisions, with necessary auxiliary services of all types, and had the support of aviation. "Panzer and motorized infantry divisions, as well as an S.S. unit" are listed by a German source as forming a part of the narrow penetration wedge which was to follow a panzer division spearhead.

In front of Von Reichenau's army was the Russian Fifth Army, which was a part of the Russian South Group of Armies under Marshal Budenny. The order of battle of the Russian Fifth Army is not known.

The German Sixth Army had on its right (southern) flank, the First Panzer Army of General von Kleist, while south of von Kleist was the Seventeenth Army of General von Stuelpnagel. These two armies later became the southern arm of the great Kiev encirclement. Further south, von Rundstedt's forces included Hungarian and Rumanian as well as German troops.

North of von Reichenau was the Center Group of Armies under General von Bock. No army of the Center Group maintained ground contact with von Reichenau after the jump-off from concentration areas; ground liaison between the two armies was prevented by the impassable Pripet marshes. East of the marshes, in the Dnieper Valley, the Second Army under von Weichs and the Second Panzer Army of Guderian later established contact with von Reichenau and became the northern arm in the Kiev encirclement.

THE PRIPET OR PINSK MARSHES AND THE ROUTES TO KIEV.

The great marshes of Western Russia are variously called Pripet, after the river which runs through but does not effectively drain them, and Pinsk, for the largest city included in their vast expanse. The term "vast" is not an exaggeration, for the marshes extend from Brest-Litovsk on the German-Russian border eastward to and beyond the Dnieper, a distance of more than 300 miles, and stretch from north to south more than 150 miles.

The marshes had a marked influence on German strategy. Such roads and railroads as existed in them were not first-class. Moreover, a demolition which would be merely a nuisance on dry land would be disastrous in a region where any detour from a road-bed meant hopeless bogging down. Consequently, the marshes could not be effectively penetrated, and were thus a natural boundary between the two groups of armies.

From his concentration area, von Reichenau had to advance toward Kiev along the southern edge of the marshes. The axis of his advance was determined by the disposition of highways and railroads.

At Kowel, the railroad line from Biala and Brest-Litovsk joined the line from Chelm and Luboml. East of Kowel, the single line led to Kiev through the southern part of the marshes, across numerous tributaries of the Pripet River. From three of the villages on this railroad, branch lines ran north or northwest toward the Pripet River or the Dnieper (see map overleaf). This road and its branches were single-track, and the gauge was different from that of German railroads.

As with the railroads, a highway from Brest-Litovsk and a highway from Luboml met at Kowel, east of which a great highway

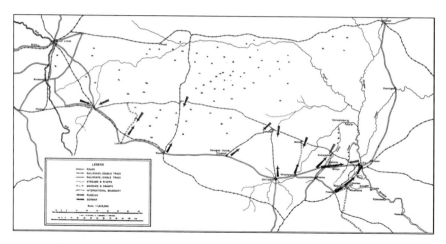

led to Kiev. This highway was of asphalt and had four traffic lanes from the old Polish-Russian border to Kiev (according to some accounts, all the way from the new German-Russian border to Kiev). This road, which was south of and approximately parallel to the Kowel-Kiev railroad, led through well-drained country and cut across the Pripet tributaries in their upper courses.

VON REICHENAU ADVANCES AND BUDENNY RETREATS.
Because of the difficulties inherent in the use of the Russian railroads, the Germans generally chose the highways for their spearheads in Russia — in this instance, the excellent Kiev highway.

The men and materiel of von Reichenau's Sixth Army had apparently been concentrated as close as possible to the border, along all-weather roads. Some of the first units to enter Russia crossed the frontier near Brest-Litovsk and advanced along the highway from Brest-Litovsk to Kowel. Others, entering further south, advanced along the highway from Luboml toward Kowel. Like the other leading units, which literally rolled into Russia on the morning of June 22, 1941, the forward units of von Reichenau's army again used the spearhead tactics which had been so successfully employed in France and moved forward with great speed, protected by superior air strength. As the Germans advanced, the Russians retreated at an average rate of some 15 miles a day.

To the German commanders, as to observers outside the battle area, the parallel with the campaign in France must have appeared striking. In each case, large areas of important territory were promptly occupied by the Germans.

The Russian withdrawal, however, was not due entirely to weakness. Beyond question, the Russians knew that the Germans had massed great quantities of men and materiel along good highways, just across the Bug. Uncertain exactly when and exactly where these massed Nazi resources would be used, the Russians apparently held their forward positions with delaying forces only and elected to make their main defensive stand many miles to the east. In this way, the Russian commanders were able to learn the direction and strength of the German thrusts before committing the Russian reserves. Even in retreating, they could learn something of German tactics. Finally, when the main engagement would take place, German lines of communication would be long and Russian lines short. These considerations, as well as the strength of the Nazi military machine, probably played a part in the rapid Russian retreat before the German armies in the 1941 campaign. Nor was the German advance made without cost. Battered vehicles abandoned by the road, dead horses, and destroyed villages told of the fury of the Russian rearguard action.

FIGHTING BETWEEN A HIGHWAY AND A RAILROAD.

Since von Kleist was on his right, von Reichenau appears to have had no difficulty on that flank as his spearhead advanced.

On the left (northern) flank, the situation was different. There was no ground contact with the nearest army of the Center Group; this army, in fact, was miles away, north of the Pripet marshes. Moreover, the Russians were in these marshes in considerable force and at once began to harass von Reichenau's left flank. Accurate and heavy Russian artillery barrages came down unexpectedly on German transport.

In spite of this harassment by Russian artillery, von Reichenau's forward troops continued to move ahead. The area taken by the spearhead troops extended not more than 2 or 3 miles on each side of the highway.

The situation on the marsh flank could not, however, be ignored.

Resistance to the Russians was left to foot-infantry troops armed with the necessary heavy weapons and artillery. At every crossroad or junction, a task force had to be constituted to cope with a Russian attack which, if neglected, might threaten the flank. A German commentator, irked by the cost of the operations, stated that a full-scale battle had to be fought for each miserable village, which was worthless in the first instance and rubble when taken.

In the battles between the troops on the highway and those on the railroads, the Germans had the advantage. They were able to move forward more troops and material on the four-lane highway than the Russians could bring up on the single-track railroad, and a Russian retreat was forced. In no case, however, was the bulk of the Russians cut off. When outgunned by superior German artillery and in danger of being flanked by the advance on the highway, the Russian troops retreated along their railroad line to the next vantage-point and again harassed the German advance.

Shortly after the campaign began, the Germans were at Kowel, the junction of the railroad line which the Russians had determined to hold and the highway on which the Germans had determined to advance. After overcoming strong Russian resistance at Kowel, the Germans again moved forward, and took in turn Luck, Rowne, Zwaihel. Soon they were at Zhitomir, an important junction some 75 miles from Kiev.

After crossing several minor streams, their forward elements reached the heights west of the Irpen River. From the summit of this high ground they could see the spires of Kiev. They were 5 miles from the outskirts and 12 miles from the heart of the city. In 20 days they had come 312 miles. With Kiev in sight, an armored division hurried down the four-lane highway toward a wooden bridge over the Irpen.

CHECK OF THE SPEARHEAD AT THE IRPEN RIVER THE GERMAN SPEARHEAD IS HALTED.

Despite the unexpected and strong Russian assaults which had harassed their advance and were still continuing against their left flank well to the rear, the Germans claim they were confident on July 12 as they started down the western (left) bank of the north-flowing Irpen. Suddenly, in front of them, the wooden bridge of the great four-lane highway was blown out by Soviet troops. Germans often make light of Russian demolitions, but this one they conceded to be perfect. There was nothing left of the bridge, and the steep west banks were under Russian fire. The armored spearheads could not cross the Irpen, and had to retreat up the hill. The delay was annoying, but (according to German sources) it did not shake the confidence of men who had advanced 312 miles in 20 days.

For 20 days they had averaged 15 miles a day; in the next 2 months, however, they were not to move a yard!

The first difficulty was the terrain. Directly in front of the Germans was the Irpen River, a natural bastion of Kiev. Here in its middle course the Irpen had dry banks, but the channel was unfordable. There were many wooded areas on the slopes, particularly on the Russian-held eastern slope, and Russian troops in these woods commanded every yard of open space between the heights on the western bank and the river. Most of the cultivated land was in tall grain, under cover of which the Germans apparently constructed field fortifications. Suburban houses, which offered many opportunities for concealment, dotted both slopes, particularly the Russian-held eastern slope. The four-lane highway cut across the Irpen and ran straight up the hill through a wood toward Kiev, but the bridge was destroyed and every foot of the roadway was under Russian fire.

The Irpen position, moreover, could not be flanked by the German advance units which were halted there. To the north near the mouth of the Irpen, the terrain was swampy, and the Russians held the rail-line in menacing strength. To the south, the upper Irpen, which widened at places into lakes, was an obstacle; and across the divide between the Irpen and the Dnieper, the Weta and the Strugna Creeks were as well defended as the Irpen.

After von Reichenau's leading elements had been halted on the west bank of the Irpen, he immediately devoted himself to a three-fold task: the consolidation of the Irpen position; the elimination of the Russian artillery which was still pounding his supply line and interfering with the bulk of the Sixth Army's movements to its new concentration area east of Zhitomir; and the protection of the Irpen position by operations on the Weta and the Strugna. The accomplishment of these tasks would have the dual result of preventing a successful Russian counterthrust and of establishing the Sixth Army in positions from which, under more favorable circumstances, a further advance might be made.

THE HALTED GERMANS DIG IN AND RECONNOITER.

Von Reichenau's forward units were much over-extended. According to German claims, these units were some 125 miles ahead of the foot-infantry divisions of their army and now had to devote themselves to holding on until the infantry divisions could come forward.

A headquarters for the defending German troops was apparently established in the little village of Milaja, just west of the Irpen, and the main body of the forward troops occupied two shallow ravines more or less parallel with the river. Fox holes were dug at once to give shelter to the troops, who were tired by their rapid advance. Construction was carried out under extreme difficulties. Any movement beyond cover brought a storm of Russian artillery fire. Russian aviators flew over the German-held houses on the west bank every 2 hours at a height stated by the Germans to be only 35 to 50 feet, dropping 5-pound bombs and machine-gunning the German positions.

There is no reference in available sources to German air reconnaissance over the Irpen position, but such reconnaissance was routine in similar situations and doubtless took place here. Ground reconnaissance was constant. From hidden positions just east of the village of Milaja, officers with camouflaged BC scopes searched the eastern banks of the Irpen. Soon a bunker was discovered. Some hours later a second bunker was detected, and finally the general course of a line of bunkers. Further observation with field glasses led to the discovery of field positions and to the conjecture that there was a tank-trap ditch behind a stockade-type fence. Numerous trucks full of men and materiel were seen to turn off into the woods on both sides of the main highway from Kiev. The Russians were evidently strengthening their already well-defended position.

THE RUSSIANS COUNTERATTACK.

In a few days the Adolph Hitler Regiment took over the position from the spearhead troops, and was later relieved by infantry at dawn on a date unknown but shortly after July 20.

But the Russian reconnaissance and intelligence had been effective. The Russians had learned precisely what was happening on the German side of the river and during the relief of units launched a strong artillery attack. During the afternoon, Russian combat patrols crossed the river on footbridges. Even though the slope on the German side of the river was level and open in comparison with the slope on the other side, Soviet advanced units, under cover of their artillery, succeeded in hiding themselves in small hollows and depressions.

At nightfall, a German battalion was ordered to regain the lost ground. On a front which extended about a mile and a half north and 2 miles south of the highway, the Germans attacked along a line about 500 yards west of and parallel to the Irpen. Under the cover afforded by fields of tall grain, they used machine guns, rifles, and hand grenades against the newly-won Russian positions under fire, however, from Russian mortars.

After a conflict which lasted about an hour and was especially violent along the highway near the blown-up bridge, the Russians were pushed back across the Irpen. The large searchlights, which the Soviets had camouflaged in the treetops, began to flare across the German-held west bank, sweeping the grain fields, and the Germans did not attempt to pursue the retreating Russians across the river. The infantrymen sought out their old fox holes east of Milaja, and an hour before dawn set up their machine guns again in the positions they had occupied before the Russians crossed the river.

THE SIXTH ARMY CONCENTRATES BEFORE KIEV.

Meanwhile, screened by the troops who had repulsed the Russian counterattack on the Irpen, the rearward combat units of von Reichenau's Army continued to move forward rapidly to positions east of Zhitomir.

The one road to Kiev had to be used by almost the entire Sixth Army; it was therefore imperative that any possible jamming and confusion be avoided. Rather than depend entirely upon guides and messengers, the Germans made great use of directional signs. At each junction there were many road markers bearing unit insignia. The signs were especially elaborate at Kotscherowo, where units turned off to protect the southern flank of the Irpen position, and at the junction south of Makarov, where units turned off to secure the northern flank. With these route markers as guides, motor vehicles left the highways without a halt for task missions against the Russian railroad positions or to move into concentration areas. Serials were formed, according to the speed of vehicles or the time a small unit was ready for moving, and the markers with division insignia were relied on to bring the subordinate units together again.

Provision had to be made for servicing and supplying advanced units, and one lane (at least between Zhitomir and Kiev) was designated for west-bound traffic, with three lanes for eastward movement of men and materiel. Over the west-bound traffic lane, transport elements of the forward units went to Zhitomir each night on missions of servicing and supply.

To sum up, the Germans, in the days following July 13, made use of the great highway to strengthen their position on the Irpen, and bring forward troops in great quantities. Some of these relieved the soldiers on the Irpen. Some were thrown off on the left flank to continue the fight for the railroad. Some moved to the South to prevent the Irpen position from being outflanked. Most of them, however, were brought just east of Zhitomir into a staging area which was almost as large as the original concentration area between Biala and Chelm on the west bank of the Bug. Supplies were also brought forward in large quantities. From this new concentration area, troops and supplies were in a position to be moved at the commander's will as operations developed.

OPERATIONS ON THE LEFT FLANK OF THE SIXTH ARMY

THE RUSSIANS CONTINUE TO THREATEN THE GERMAN LEFT FLANK.

While von Reichenau in the days following July 13 was strengthening his position on the Irpen and was bringing forward the bulk of the Sixth Army into its new concentration area east of Zhitomir, Russian artillery was still active on his north (left) flank. The Russians on the railroad had apparently not retreated further eastward than Korosten, and Russian artillery was now dangerously near the new concentration area east of Zhitomir. Accordingly, von Reichenau determined to secure at any cost his exposed left flank, and launched a vigorous assault on the Russian position at Korosten. The railway junction here was defended by the Russians with bitter determination, and it fell into German hands only after hard fighting; again, the Russians retreated northwest and east along the railroad lines.

THE BATTLE FOR ANDREJEVKA.

By July 23, the Germans had mopped up Korosten and other neighborhoods to the east, and now determined to take Andrejevka. Many details in regard to the struggle for this village are available and are believed to be typical.

For the Andrejevka engagement, German forward units apparently left the Zhitomir-Kiev highway at the junction near Makarov. During the night of July 22-23, several artillery battalions and a smoke battalion moved up under cover of darkness, and took their positions less than three-quarters of a mile from the infantry front line. At 0430, light and heavy field howitzers, 100-mm guns and 180-mm mortars opened fire against the Soviet field fortifications which German observers had detected on the southern edge of Andrejevka. At the same time, German smoke shells fell among the Russian field positions and spread a thick veil of smoke just in front of the village.

The heavy fire preparation, the laying of the smoke screen, and the beginning of the infantry advance had been coordinated. The Russians were blinded; neither their forward infantrymen nor their observers in observation posts could see more than five or six yards through the thick smoke. Unobserved, the German infantrymen left their positions of readiness and rushed across the open terrain toward Andrejevka, whole infantry companies reaching the edge of the village with hardly the loss of a man. The Russians were unable to check the German advance with their heavy weapons, because their firing was based on data obtained before the laying of the smoke screen.

The smoke screen had been launched under ideal weather conditions and remained for a long time.

As soon as the Soviet observers could see through the gradually disappearing smoke, they directed fire against the German attacking infantry. However, the German forward artillery observers quickly informed their batteries of the location of the Soviet artillery and heavy weapons positions. These positions were at once shelled heavily, and soon became silent.

The German infantrymen then entered Andrejevka, which consisted of many field positions, all excellently camouflaged and all liberally provided with machine guns and mortars. Houses and barns had been equipped for defense. The Russian positions were in many cases connected by cleverly arranged trench systems.

THE THREAT TO THE LEFT FLANK IS REMOVED.

The engagement at Andrejevka was basically a struggle for the Korosten-Kiev railway line, which passed a mile or two to the north. With the German capture of this village, following the capture of Korosten and Malin, this vital railroad, except for a short suburban portion near Kiev, was in German hands. The Russians who had threatened von Reichenau's left flank withdrew now to assist in the defense of Kiev. No information is available as to their line of retreat; but most of them probably fell back along the railroad to the strongly held position east of the Irpen. The new Russian front line north of the Zhitomir-Kiev highway became something like the top half of the letter "C".

Overcoming the Russian resistance along the railroad reduced the threat of a Russian flank attack from the north. Few roads and railways led through the Pripet marshes toward the new German positions, and the Germans instead of the Russians were now aided by the fact that a slight demolition could render a whole area impassable.

Von Reichenau had not only secured his left flank; he was also getting into position to make contact (previously denied him by the Pripet marshes) with von Bock, whose Second Army and Second Armored Army were soon to move down from the north.

OPERATIONS ON THE RIGHT OF THE SIXTH ARMY

A CORPS MOVES TO SUPPORT THE RIGHT FLANK.

While elements on the northern flank of von Reichenau's army were attacking Russian positions on the railroad north of the Zhitomir-Kiev highway, one of his corps was assigned a mission to the south. The mission of this corps was not only to assist in securing the Irpen position but to put von Reichenau's army into areas from which an assault upon Kiev could be made when the situation permitted.

The German units destined to take part in the large-scale operations south of the Irpen position turned off the main Zhitomir-Kiev highway at Kotscherowo, and proceeded in a southeasterly direction by way of Brusilov to Fastov. German panzer and motorized infantry divisions went first along the paved road, which stopped at Fastov, some 40 miles southwest of Kiev. Beyond Fastov, the troops had to advance toward their new positions along ordinary roads, which had been turned into mud by a three-day rain.

On a front of some 12 miles running from southeast to northwest astride the Fastov-Vasilkov-Kiev road, five infantry divisions were moved up to establish prepared assembly areas from which an attack was to be made later against Kiev. Fastov was the center of combat for the entire sector, since it was the only practical road to Vasilkov, the one city of any size between Fastov and Kiev. There were regimental assembly areas on each side of this road.

Two villages, Gelenovka on the left and Marjanovka on the right, flanked the roadway some distance in front of these assembly areas, and as the Germans approached these villages they encountered difficult terrain, for the Strugna had many tributary creeks with steep slopes. The two villages had, moreover, been very heavily fortified by the Russians, and here again, as north of the Zhitomir-Kiev highway, the Germans were compelled to use their heavy weapons and expend themselves in force against unimportant localities which the Russians had transformed into fortresses.

THE GERMANS USE DIVE BOMBERS AND TANKS IN CAPTURING THE VILLAGE OF GELENOVKA.

The German heavy artillery had been moved into position, apparently south of Fastov, and by July 30 von Reichenau felt that his southern corps was ready to launch an attack toward Kiev. The attack was made at 0400 on a 12-mile front. Artillery concentrations fell on Gelenovka and Marjanovka—and at the same instant similarly heavy Russian artillery attacks were directed upon the German positions. The Germans learned later from prisoners that the Russians had, by an unusual coincidence, made their plans for an attack upon the German positions at this same hour.

Under the cover of fire by their artillery, German infantry troops moved into positions of readiness at the bottom of the small valley in front of Gelenovka. During this movement, they were under fire from Russian artillery.

Either by previous plan or because of the unexpectedly heavy Russian artillery fire, the Germans sent in eight dive bombers at 0530. The German and the Russian artillery fire ceased as the planes appeared. These dive bombers released their bombs at an altitude of about 450 feet. A decrease in Russian fire indicated that Soviet observation posts and guns had been hit by the bombs.

The advancing German infantry, however, had to cross broad fields of ripe grain before arriving at the edge of the village. In accordance with their customary tactics, the Soviets had taken advantage of the cover afforded by the grain and, digging deeply into the black soil, had constructed an elaborate system of field positions to protect the village. Russian machine-gun fire from flanking positions, as well as carelessly directed German infantry fire, increased the difficulties of the forward German units as they moved through the grain fields. There was heavy hand-to-hand fighting for the Soviet machine-gun and rifle nests. Finally, the leading German units reached the edge of Gelenovka. There again machine guns, rifles, and hand grenades were used on both sides in close combat in front of the village.

In spite of bitter and incessant fighting from 0400, Gelenovka was still held by the Russians shortly before sunset. At this time, German armored assault artillery advanced through lanes among the halted forward elements and charged into the village, firing in every direction from which resistance appeared. Riflemen followed closely and beat down any resistance not broken by the assault artillery. At sunset Gelenovka was finally captured. The exhausted infantry sat at the side of the road amid dead Soviet soldiers, crushed horses, and burned vehicles and watched a stream of Russian prisoners led to the rear.

According to German sources, an equally severe struggle was necessary to secure possession of other villages, including Marjanovka. When Marjanovka was taken, the Germans felt that they had entered the outer protective ring of the positions in front of Kiev.

THE GERMANS ARE STOPPED AT WETA CREEK BY RUSSIAN DEPLOYMENT IN DEPTH.

On July 31, German troops worked forward from Marjanovka toward Vasilkov, the only city on the road to Kiev from the south. German observers with glasses sought for any possible show of hostile resistance in the tall grain. Infantrymen combed the grain fields and the steep slopes of the Strugna tributaries.

The Russians harassed the German advance by artillery fire; however, they evacuated the inhabitants of Vasilkov, and did not defend that city. The Germans entered the town, established headquarters, and dug in around the outskirts to protect the units and supplies which were brought up.

During the forenoon of August 1, the leading German elements continued beyond Vasilkov in close pursuit of the Russians. After passing through several villages and crossing several swamps, the

Germans, encountering increased opposition, approached the Weta, which the Russians had determined to hold. Russian artillery and mortar shelling of the German forward positions was extremely heavy on August 1, 2, and 3.

In front of the Germans and across the Weta, the Russians had constructed a semicircular line of bunkers similar to those further north along the Irpen River. The Germans at once began efforts to force these positions. At dawn on August 3, a young lieutenant succeeded in leading his platoon into the valley through a ravine obscured from the enemy. The platoon crossed the Weta and surprised a hostile security group located behind wire obstructions and an antitank ditch. Although accurate Russian shellfire prevented this platoon from holding its position, the observations reported by the lieutenant formed the basis for his battalion commander's attack. During the evening of August 3, German heavy weapons units, varying from heavy mortars to light field howitzers, completed their movement into positions in front of the Weta bunkers. Fire began at once, and hits were registered on positions located by observers in advance posts.

On August 4 at 0400, German artillery opened a heavy concentration of fire against Russian fortifications in the woods across the Weta. Three Russian bunkers received direct hits. After 45 minutes of continuous firing, there was a lull of five minutes, and at 0450 the German shelling was renewed with increased intensity. Smoke mortars next went into action; their shells exploded in front of and between enemy bunkers, and covered the center of the valley with a smoke cloud. Artillery fire was continued. The commander of a German infantry battalion leaped out of his cover, led his companies down the slope, through the knee-deep Weta, and across a 70-yard open space to a lane cut through the Wire entanglements by the bridgehead platoon. Fortunately for the Germans, the bunker which protected the antitank ditch just beyond the wire had been put out of action by a mortar.

After crossing the antitank ditch, the right flank rifle company encountered another band of wire entanglements. Pioneers rushed to the front and cut a lane, through which a second special group of pioneers moved against the bunker on the right, bursting it open with two concentrated explosive charges. Then the flame throwers squirted their liquid fire into the hatchways, and a black smoke cloud obscured the view for some minutes. The Germans pushed on into the forest and found numerous abandoned field positions dug deeply into the earth. Their artillery fire had destroyed Russian resistance in that particular area. In places, the forest was a jumble of giant craters, broken trees, and torn branches. The air was full of dust mingled with the smell of exploded shells. A rolling barrage of German artillery, directed by observers with the leading elements, lifted just ahead of the Germans advancing through the forest. Finally the Russians were pushed out of their last positions in this area, which was over 100 yards inside the forest and a little more than a mile from the creek.

Simultaneously, other Russian bunker positions were penetrated, not only here, but on the front of the entire corps attacking on the south. The Russian fortifications were arranged in great depth, however, and this corps, while it had scored minor gains, could not effect a break-through.

Under heavy Russian fire the German riflemen lay on either side of the road in deep trenches which protected them from hostile shell splinters. They were surrounded by ankle-deep mud, and stretched pieces of canvas over themselves for shelters. They did not shave or wash for days. The field kitchens were several miles in the rear, and by the time meals could be served the food was cold. But, in spite of difficulties; the Germans held their position in spite of strong Russian counterattacks. They thought, according to their own accounts, that they would reach Kiev in 2 or 3 days. However, they remained in their positions, 12 miles from the heart of the city, and for a number of weeks made no advance against the determined Soviet resistance.

In the meantime the Germans strengthened their positions, turned Vasilkov into a headquarters town, and brought up supplies and reinforcements again by an all-out attack, which made no appreciable headway.

VON REICHENAU'S HALTED ARMY BECOMES THE HOLDING ATTACK OF THE KIEV ENCIRCLEMENT OPERATION

The situation before Kiev was finally resolved in September by events many miles away, both south and north. In the south, von Stuelpnegel had thrown a bridge across the river below Kremenchug, (see Tactical and Technical Trends No. 7 p. 40), and still nearer German forces had established bridgeheads across the Dnieper at Kanev, Rjishchev, and Tripole. Thus the west bank of the lower Dnieper was in German hands.

In the north, von Kleist had crossed the Desna near Novgorod-Seversky. Also, on the northern flank, a German advance to the northeast had forced the Russians out of Garnostaipol and across the Dnieper. The more northern elements of von Reichenau's Army had also established connection with von Weichs's army which had advanced north of the Pripet marshes, and had turned southward and crossed the Desna.

If the Germans had planned to take Kiev by a frontal attack, they had failed. Von Reichenau's army in two months of effort made no appreciable headway on the Irpen and on the Weta. The Germans had, however, dug themselves in so that they could not be easily thrown back. Whether the Germans had planned to take Kiev and had failed, or whether they had planned merely to secure strong positions before that city, they were now ready to become the holding attack in the envelopment which followed.

On September 17 at 0630 von Reichenau, once more began his attack on the Russian positions. As usual, violent artillery bombardment, assisted by dive bombers, paved the way for assaults with mortars, machine guns, hand grenades, and other weapons. The Russians again defended villages so stubbornly that each village outside of Kiev was destroyed. Because of the closing of the trap by armored troops far to the east of Kiev, however, the Russians had to cease their resistance, and withdraw across the Dnieper River. The city was captured by the Germans on September 19. Despite their heroic 10 weeks of resistance to the Germans in front of Kiev, the outflanking operations of von Bock from the north and of von Rundstedt from the south had forced the Kiev defenders into a disastrous position. The Russian soldiers who had fought so valiantly were withdrawn across the Dnieper, but were not able to escape from the trap which closed around at least four and possibly five of Budenny's armies.

11. THE GERMAN ADVANCE FROM THE NORTH: KIEV OPERATION

Tactical and Technical Trends, No. 16, January 14th 1943

INTRODUCTION

Upon entering Russia on June 22, 1941, the German Center Group of Armies under Marshal von Bock had little difficulty in effecting a double encirclement of the cities of Bialystock and Minsk. After this victory, von Bock again pushed his group of armies eastward and effected the encirclement of Smolensk, a strategically important city known as the "western gate of Moscow". Despite the fact that the capture of Smolensk (August 6) had proved costly, von Bock again thrust forward—this time apparently in an attempt to encircle Viazma. The fighting was bitter. The German Second Panzer Army was cut off by the Russians and was rescued only by a lavish use of air power. The spearhead of the Center Group of Armies was definitely brought to a halt by Marshal Timoshenko before Moscow.

THE KIEV OPERATION

After the failure of the German Center Group of Armies to make further gains toward Moscow, and after the similar failures of the North Group of Armies approaching Leningrad and the South Group before Kiev, the Germans initiated the great double encirclement, which is generally referred to as the Kiev Operation. It is not known whether this operation was envisioned before June 22, or whether it was attempted as the only large operation possible after the failure of the frontal attacks against the three great cities.

In any event, the plan was as follows: Kiev was to be enveloped and as many as possible of Marshall Budenny's armies were to be trapped and destroyed in a gigantic double pincers envelopment, or wedge and trap operation (see map at end of article). The holding attack, and the two southern pincers arms or the southern wedge were to be from the South Group of Armies under Marshal von Rundstedt. Von Reichenau's Sixth Army, which had been halted on the Irpen River west of Kiev, was to launch the holding attack. The Seventeenth Army of von Stuelpnegel and the First Panzer Army of von Kleist were to constitute the two southern pincers arms of the southern wedge. The wedge from the north was to be formed from the Center Group of Armies of Marshal von Bock. The Second Panzer Army under General Guderian and the Second Army under General von Weichs constituted the northern pincers arms. The outer pair of pincers, the two Panzer Armies, was to close about 125 miles east of Kiev.

Of course, no two double pincers or wedge-and-trap (Keil and Kessel) operations are exactly alike, but the Kiev operation may be regarded as typical. The scheme of maneuver was basically the same on both flanks. The outer pincers arm (a panzer army) drove forward to meet the approaching arm. As the armored spearhead moved on, small task forces were thrown off on the outer flank for security, and on the inner flank to drive the Russians toward troops of the inner pincers arm (composed chiefly of infantry divisions) or against natural obstacles, or to envelop them, and, in any case, to destroy them. Simultaneously with the advance of the armored pincers arm, infantry armies broke through to form the inner pincers and devoted themselves primarily to the annihilation of pockets of troops cut off by the outer Panzer pincers arms. To sum up, between the jaws of the closing pincers—in this case two pairs, an outer and an inner—the enemy is crushed. Or, in the other figure of speech, when the wedges meet, the trap is closed and the enemy is exposed to total annihilation.

TWO "MOSCOW" ARMIES TURN TO THE SOUTH

The southern flank of von Bock's armies extended from the apex of his advance at Roslavl through Rogachev to the Pripet Marshes. On the eastern end of this long flank, Guderian's Second Panzer Army faced to the south and von Weich's Second Army which had advanced in the rear of Guderian's forces, also faced south on the western end of this flank. The mission of both armies was to drive southward, capture the city of Gomel, trap the Russian forces in that area, and seize bridgeheads across the Desna. The Second Panzer Army was to protect the east flank of the southward moving forces from Russian counterattack. The Second Army was to establish contact across the east end of the Pripet Marshes with von Reichenau's Sixth Army, the most northern army of von Rundstedt's South Group of Armies. The German advance was in general over thickly wooded and marshy terrain. Prior to August 12, the Germans were advancing on the entire Russian front.

THE EASTERN ARM OF THE DOUBLE PINCERS IN THE NORTH

At the beginning of the Kiev Operation, the Second Panzer Army was in the vicinity of Roslavl, a railroad junction on the old Post Road which led south from Smolensk. Its main body apparently advanced south from Roslavl, over the only motor road leading in that direction. Soon after the advance in the new direction began, another element moved southwest, probably with the double purpose of cutting Russian supply lines and shielding more closely the Second Army's left flank. Concerning this advance, there are no available details from Russian sources, but German claims, that the Second Panzer Army rolled back the Russians by a flanking movement to the west before reaching the Gomel-Bryansk railroad, would indicate that the Panzer elements left the south road at Mglin and pushed toward Gomel. The Panzer elements which occupied Chernigov probably left the Post Road further south at Starodub, but some or all of them may have left the Post Road at Mglin and may have turned south from the Mglin-Gomel road.

The Germans state that Unecha was bitterly contested. No further details are available, except that the Second Panzer Army captured the junction and pushed on to the south. Another German source states that on August 17, there was a tank battle about 130 kilometers (80 miles) south of Roslavl. This was probably the fight for the Unecha junction.

Unlike the road followed by the Second Army from Mogilev to Gomel and thence to Kiev, the Second Panzer Army's road via Unecha to Novgorod Syeversk was not a first-class road, and the available German accounts of the fighting deal in large part with bad road conditions brought about by heavy rains. According to a German source, the vehicles literally had to grind their way through deep mud. The ground was so soft, according to this source, that log roads constructed by the Germans were pressed far into the mud and rendered almost useless by the weight of the supply elements of the German columns. Since the season was summer, it appears that the drying-out of roads was rapid; in any event, Novgorod Syeversk on the Desna was reached. Here bridgeheads were at once established south of the Desna, and the Second Panzer Army was rapidly reorganized and made ready for its part in the Kiev encirclement.

THE WESTERN ARM

At the time of its right turn to the south, the Second Army under von Weichs was apparently concentrated about 100 miles west of Roslavl in the Mogilev-Bobruisk area. A part of this army drove south toward Gomel over a first-class road paralleling and east of the Dnieper. As in the case of the advance of the Second Panzer Army, no details are available concerning this drive to the south.

According to German sources, a flank attack was launched on Gomel by troops which advanced via Jlobin (in some accounts south of Jlobin) and struggled through the Pripet Marshes. Because of the difficult terrain and lack of roads, these troops, however, were probably a relatively small part of the Second Army. No road (according to available maps) leads directly from the Bobruisk area to Gomel. Even the roundabout routes were over poor roads. The road from Rogachev to Jlobin was worse than second-class; no road led all the way from Jlobin to Gorval; and the road from Gorval to Gomel was second-class or worse. Thus German troops, by whatever route they approached Gomel from the west, faced bad road conditions.

The Second Army encircled and destroyed pockets of Russians at Rogachev and Jlobin and soon struck at Gomel. Despite a strong

Russian counterattack, the maneuver, which was apparently an envelopment, was completely successful. The defenders were trapped and the city fell on August 19. According to a German source, infantry, artillery, and engineers had all played major roles; prisoners numbered 84,000; 144 tanks, 949 guns, 38 airplanes, and 2 armored trains were captured.

It appears that von Reichenau's final campaign for seizing the Brest Litovsk-Kiev railroad was not begun until after the success of the Second Army's drive was indicated. Those Russians on the railroad who could not get back to Kiev tried to escape through the marshes and across the Dnieper to Chernigov, but elements of the Second Panzer Army, which presumably had moved over the Starodub-Chernigov road, were already in that city, and the retreating Russians were trapped. Since Chernigov dominated several routes to the east, its loss was a serious blow to the Russians.

PREPARATIONS ARE COMPLETE

By August 21, the Germans held all territory north of the Desna, and both of the northern pincers arms were ready for the final phase of the operation, the advance southward below the Desna into the Russian-held Kiev salient.

While the Second Army and the Second Panzer Army were crossing the Desna into their newly established bridgeheads, other related events had been occurring. Northwest of Kiev, the holding forces of von Reichenau drew nearer to the city after the defeat of the Russians along the Brest Litovsk-Kiev railroad. Von Reichenau's forces had also approached nearer to Kiev on his south flank and, though unsuccessful in an apparent effort at taking that city, had developed strong bunker lines and other defenses behind which troops had been brought up for the Kiev holding attack. This attack, coordinated with the operations south of the Desna, was now launched. Simultaneously in the south, von Rundstedt's South Group of armies had on August 31 thrown a bridge across the Dnieper River below Kiev at Kremenchug, and had effected crossings at other places. The troops of von Kleist's First Panzer Army became the outer pincers arm and the troops of von Stuelpnegel's Seventeenth Army became the inner pincers arm of the envelopment from the south.

THE SECOND ARMY CROSSES THE DESNA

No details are available in regard to the advance south of the Desna by the German Second Army, but the road-net and the general tactical situation would indicate that some elements drove south by Kozelets toward Kiev and that others, further east, drove toward Priluki. Each of these roads was an admirable route for the Kessel part of the wedge-and-trap (Keil and Kessel) maneuver. The road via Kozelets for miles commanded the double-track Kiev-Moscow railroad, and the junction at Brovari commanded every highway available for a withdrawal from Kiev. The road via Priluki at and south of Piryatin likewise intersected important Russian roads and railroads, and continued southeast of Lubni (see below).

THE SECOND PANZER ARMY CROSSES THE DESNA

The Second Panzer Army crossed the Desna just beyond Novgorod Syeversk, the first large town inside the northern boundary of the Ukraine. The Desna, which is some 655 miles long, is the largest tributary of the Dnieper.

The river was defended by strong and extensive fortifications along the eastern and southern banks. German sources state that the bunker walls here consisted of two timbers, each 12 inches thick, with an intervening space of 24 inches filled with sand.

As the Germans advanced, the service of engineers was constantly needed. The Germans had to repair a damaged bridge across the Desna and had to build a ponton bridge over the Seim.

At Konotop where the railroad from Kiev to Moscow intersected a north-south highway, the Russians resisted stubbornly, for they realized that the loss of Konotop would not only prevent supplies from being sent to the retreating armies in the trap, but would imperil the retreat of these armies from the trap. However, the Germans captured the city and the outer armored pincers arm was free to advance the remainder of the distance across the northern half of the

Kiev salient. As the advance elements moved forward, other troops came up and held the town and protected the rear.

After the Germans took Konotop, the Second Panzer Army drove straight across country toward Romni. A very heavy rain began to fall as the leading battalion entered the town. It rained continuously on September 11 and 12, and German armored vehicles had great difficulty moving in the mud. Large towing-machines and caterpillar tractors were the only vehicles which could pull out the heavy trucks loaded with fuel, ammunition, and supplies. At times the supply elements were completely out of contact with the combat elements. Even the engineers, according to the Germans, were powerless because of the mud. Drivers used tree trunks and branches, wire rolls, and wooden fences to make wheels take hold, and yard by yard the vehicles moved forward.

The bad weather did not last long, and the main body of Germans reached Romni. German tanks drove through the town and across the first bridge beyond without much trouble. However, the Russians opened fire on the unarmored vehicles following in the rear. A second bridge, at the exit of the town, was stubbornly defended by snipers with automatic weapons in cleverly built positions along the steep embankment on the far side of the river. German engineers and riflemen finally drove the Russians out of the emplacements by going around and attacking from the rear. Then the armored spearhead moved on towards Lokhvitsa, farther to the south.

As the Germans moved south they met, with ever greater frequency, Russian troops attempting to flee from the trap, the closing of which was by now obvious to the Russian commander. Some Russians escaped, but the rapid closing of the trap caught most of the Kiev defenders inside.

THE NORTHERN WEDGE MEETS THE SOUTHERN

As the Germans approached Lokhvitsa, they captured three bridges but encountered resistance. The Soviet forces made a counterattack supported by antiaircraft guns using direct fire. Some tanks and a truck with quadruple-mounted machine guns attempted to take the bridges from the Germans. These Russian vehicles approached to within 300 yards and then their attack slowed down in the face of the fire of German antitank guns and howitzers. Since they drove back but did not destroy the attacking Russians, the Germans protected their positions by laying mine fields. On Friday, September 12, some of the German armored vehicles entered the town, and on Saturday the 13th, they pushed on to villages only some 25 miles from the northward-moving tanks of the First Panzer Army of General von Kleist.

The closing of the armored pincers was to take place without delay. On Sunday, September 14, a strong reconnaissance element of the Mark Brandenburg Panzer Division from the Berlin area, cut the Kiev-Kharkov railroad, over which supplies were brought for the Soviet armies in this area. This panzer division continued to advance southward. By this time the advance elements of a Panzer division from the Rundstedt South Group of Armies had penetrated as far north as Lubin.

As the northern arm moved south over the last miles, it encountered Russian trucks and horse-drawn wagons. These were dispersed by fire and the advance continued. A German reconnaissance plane was overhead. Radio messages were constant. Shortly after 1430, the valley of the Sula was entered. River crossings were necessary, and dangerous highway defenses were encountered, but the heights at Luka were reached at 1620. Two hours later the advance elements reached a demolished bridge on a small tributary of the Sula. Across the stream was an armored reconnaissance detachment of a Vienna regiment belonging to the First Panzer Army of the South Group of Armies. The armored pincers arms from the north had met the one from the south. The advance continued on to Lubni.

While the advance continued south from Lokhvitsa to Lubni, a spearhead from the South Group of Armies were being driven north from Mirgorod along the highway, to Lokhvitsa. No difficulties were encountered, since elements of the Mark Brandenburg Division were already waiting for the advancing elements of the Vienna Division. The wedge operation was completed.

THE KESSEL

According to German practice, the two outer encircling Panzer arms threw out on their outer flanks enough tank elements to prevent a breakthrough by any Russian forces to the east. Troops of the inner pincers arms were enabled to devote themselves exclusively to entrapping and capturing the Russians. The Second Army elements referred to above .as moving via Kozelets and Priluki had the help of Von Stuelpnegel's Seventeenth Army which moved up from Kremenchug. Crossing the Dnieper at Kiev, von Reichenau's Sixth Army also attacked the Russians who were attempting a withdrawal. Hemmed in on all sides, the Russians were soon defeated. The German mopping-up maneuvers apparently consisted chiefly in minor wedge and trap operations in any area where German forces could either encircle a body of Russians or pin it against a natural obstacle. The Germans pronounced the Kiev operation officially concluded on September 22, and claimed that 665,000 Russians, including four or five of Budenny's armies, were captured.

The figure, however, seems excessively large unless (as is German custom) all able-bodied men in the district were counted as prisoners of war. In fact a German account intimates that women as well as men were counted in the total: "female riflemen.... refused to be regarded as civilians. They were soldiers and could shoot machine guns and pistols like a man. So they had to march with the male prisoners."

CONCLUSIONS

Several conclusions can be drawn from the Kiev encirclement:
(1) A large encirclement operation is more than a simple advance by armored troops. It generally begins by an initial breakthrough toward some definite point, the occupation of which will threaten a vital line of communications.
(2) Secondary pincers movements may be expected at any point as the operation develops.

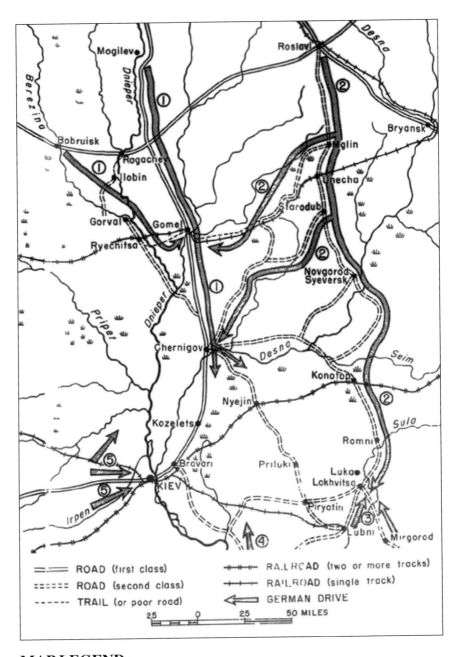

MAP LEGEND:

1. *Approximate routes of the Second Army of von Weichs.*
2. *Approximate routes of the Second Panzer Army of Guderian.*
3. *Spearheads of the First Panzer Army of von Kleist.*
4. *Spearhead of the Seventeenth Army of von Stuelpnegel.*
5. *The holding attack of the Sixth Army of von Reichenau.*

(3) Emergencies must be met by subordinate commanders on the spot by intelligent action in harmony with the general plan.

(4) Superiority in the air, superior mobility on the ground, and smoothly functioning radio communications are absolutely essential.

(5) Supply and vehicle maintenance agencies must be prepared to cope with unusual and often precarious situations. Security must be carefully planned and vigorously executed.

(6) From German accounts it would appear that Panzer forces often operate with calculated recklessness and without flank protection. These forces in fact operate ahead of the main body, but a study of an operation will usually reveal that the exposed flank of the rapidly moving units is protected by natural obstacles or by adequate forces assigned to this mission, or by both.

(7) An important principle of the successful encirclement is the application of greatly superior combat power at decisive points. The German plan was to immobilize, surround, and annihilate units before they could be thrown into action.

(8) The fundamental steps in the German plan of operations may be summed up as follows: first, to locate the enemy through reconnaissance and espionage; second, to disrupt enemy communications by air power; third, to concentrate decisively superior strength at vital points, with full use of secrecy, deception and speed of execution; fourth, to encircle and annihilate the hostile forces.

12. GERMAN TACTICS IN THE FINAL PHASES AT KHARKOV

Tactical and Technical Trends, No. 12, November 19th 1942

In the Russian offensive against Kharkov in May their forces became overextended and were encircled by the Germans. Here they encountered several innovations in the system of hasty fortifications which the Germans threw up to prevent a breakout. These defenses were built around the basic infantry strongpoints, but the way the Germans used their combined arms and armored equipment is revealing.

Figures 1 and 2 in the accompanying sketches overleaf outline the systems set up by the Germans around the encircled Russian forces. The sites of the defense areas were selected so that each island of resistance could mutually support the ones adjacent to it.

Each island or center of resistance was formed by three concentric rings. Within the center ring, self-propelled artillery capable of all-around fire was emplaced. In the next outer ring, tanks were camouflaged and embedded in the ground so that they served as pillboxes for their machine guns and other armament. The outer ring was formed by entrenched infantry units provided with their normal infantry weapons, including antitank guns and mortars.

Wire entanglements were laid between the embedded vehicles of the second ring and along the channels of fire of the infantry weapons. Clever signaling devices such as cowbells and self-igniting firecrackers were hung on the wires and nearby bushes to warn of an enemy approach at night.

In the gaps between centers of resistance, minefields were laid and charted, and high-trajectory weapons laid to cover defiladed areas.

Outside this system of defensive areas which encircled the Russian troops, mobile combat teams were located, ready to rush to any part of the circumference that might be threatened either from within or without.

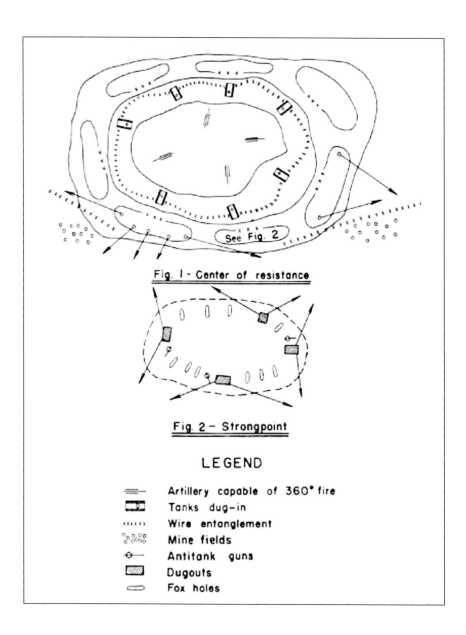

Fig. 1 - Center of resistance

See Fig. 2

Fig 2 - Strongpoint

LEGEND

☰	Artillery capable of 360° fire
▭	Tanks dug-in
······	Wire entanglement
°₀°₀°	Mine fields
⊙—	Antitank guns
▨	Dugouts
⬯	Fox holes

13. NEW GERMAN METHODS AGAINST RUSSIAN WINTER CONDITIONS

Tactical and Technical Trends,
No. 12, November 19th 1942

No Russian campaign could safely be undertaken without taking into account the challenge to an invading army's staying power to meet the hardships and danger imposed by "General Winter."

It is reported that the German Wehrmacht intends to make large-scale use this winter of diesel oil as a radiator fluid for motorized equipment in Russia, to protect motors both against low temperature and penetrating winds. Diesel oil will be used in normal motors which require draining during long stops and require the heating of oil before motors can be restarted, and also used in those few motors now being equipped with built-in warming apparatus. The use of oil was determined after experiments revealed that it has a freezing point below -40 degrees Centigrade, a boiling point higher than water, does not corrode motors or radiators, leaves no residue, and is more readily available and transportable on the Eastern Front than other chemical cooling fluids.

Since no advance preparations had been made last year to meet such weather conditions, German equipment became unusable, or usable only with great difficulty in many sectors. This experience, plus study and improvement of Russian methods and apparatus, have enabled German engineers to make the following adjustments:

(a) German batteries are too small for eastern winter conditions, and in fact electric starting becomes impossible at -30 degrees Centigrade. Since it is impossible to replace batteries, the use of other starting equipment has become necessary. Heating devices for batteries for ordinary operation have been installed in the form of small benzine lamps in closed battery compartments.

(b) Heavy motors, chilled by cold and steady penetrating wind, are impossible to start without preheating the cooling fluid and oil. This was done last winter by hot-air heating devices improvised on the spot, as well as by draining and warming the cooling fluid. On the other hand, many Soviet heavy motors were equipped with built-in auxiliary starting motors, which, after running about 30 minutes and heating the cooling fluid were able to start the main motor. Germany has adopted an improved version of this Soviet development for use on new equipment.

(c) Germany's main desire was to develop a method whereby heavy motors could be started almost immediately. This requires heating of both cooling fluid and oil before starting. The Russian auxiliary motor has been refined and improved by the addition of an oil-line break-valve to the water line, which enables the heating of both oil and fluid within a very few minutes operation, and thus the main motor can be started in but a fraction of the time required by the original Russian equipment. This improvement is stated to operate most satisfactorily.

(d) With special fuel, the Otto motored equipment can still make use of electric starting apparatus.

Diesel oil makes most satisfactory cooling fluid for winter use in all motorized equipment including that started mechanically or by hand.

14. TANK WARFARE IN STREETS

Tactical and Technical Trends,
No. 14, December 17th 1942

The following comments were compiled from observations of the recent tank battles in the streets of Stalingrad.

The German commander held the mass of his tanks in the rear areas, throwing only small groups of from three to five tanks down any one street.

The accompanying infantry precedes the tanks, and only when the surrounding buildings are overcome do the tanks advance. Thus, the best defense against tanks in street warfare is to place the most experienced automatic riflemen out in front.

It is necessary to deploy tanks in the defense so that they will form a dense crossfire, enfilade, and flanking fire. This can best be obtained by controlling the street intersections. Infantry and artillery must be disposed in the intervals between, and in front of, the tanks.

It is desirable that tanks held in reserve be assembled near intersections.

Tanks should be controlled by radio. Messenger service is too slow and telephone wire is too easily broken.

The infantry commander must be located near the tank commander, and the commanders of the smaller rifle units must be with the commanders of individual tanks. The rifle commanders locate targets for the tanks, and correct and change their fire from one target to another.

15. RUSSIAN TANK CAMOUFLAGE IN WINTER

Tactical and Technical Trends, No. 17, January 28th 1943

The following report is a translation of a Russian article on tank camouflage in winter. The original article was written by a colonel in the Russian Army.

a. General

Winter camouflage of tanks presents a problem with certain special features, created on the one hand by the general winter background, and on the other by weather conditions which greatly affect the tanks themselves and their employment under combat conditions. In winter the change in the operational characteristics of the tanks and in the conditions of employing them in combat will influence the work to be done toward camouflaging them.

Winter conditions (as has been shown by combat experience) create considerable difficulties for the camouflage of tank units. In winter the principal characteristics of a region are its uniform white background, a lack of outline, and an almost complete absence of color. The only exceptions are small settlements, woods, and thick underbrush. Forests whose dense foliage provides perfect concealment in the summertime lose their masking qualities completely in the winter. In winter, on an even, white blanket of snow, camouflage is very difficult. Almost all methods of camouflage employed in summer prove inapplicable. It is necessary to make wide use of special winter covering for the vehicles, and to paint them with winter paint: all one color (protective coat) or in large spots (disruptive).

In winter, tracks made by moving vehicles can be easily recognized, not only from the air but also from high ground observation posts. The removal of tracks left by tanks is the personal responsibility of the commander of the tank units and of the crews.

The presence of a blanket of snow, which is often very thick, greatly reduces the mobility of tanks, and as a result reduces the possibility of tanks appearing quickly and suddenly from directions unexpected by the enemy. Tanks cannot go through more than 3 inches of snow without appreciable loss of speed. The deepest snow through which a tank can go is 3 feet; for practical purposes tanks can operate in 1 1/2 feet of snow. It is apparent that these conditions greatly reduce the possibility of using approach routes concealed from enemy observation. Snow makes it necessary for tanks to employ existing roads, which means that they must engage in all their combat operations in those parts of the terrain which are under the special observation of the enemy.

An important winter factor from the point of view of concealment is the longer period of darkness, which helps to conceal the movement and disposition of tanks, provided, of course, that all camouflage measures are carefully observed.

Another winter factor which may be considered important from the point of view of camouflage and concealment is the greater cloudiness of the sky, which hinders reconnaissance activity by enemy aviation and sometimes stops it completely. Then too, tanks may make use of snowstorms which produce conditions of bad visibility and audibility, and as a result tend to lessen vigilance on the part of enemy observation posts.

b. Tank Painting

In winter, tanks are painted all white when the aim is to avoid observation, and in two colors with large spots when the aim is to avoid identification. As a rule, all-white paint is employed in level, open country characterized by a lack of variegated color. Two-color disruptive winter paint is used where the ground presents a variety of color, where there are forests, underbrush, small settlements, thawed patches of earth, etc.

One-color camouflage paint is applied to all parts of the tank in one or two coats. For the paint, zinc white or tytanium white is used only with an oil base, and slight amounts of ultramarine coloring. For the lack of anything better, the tanks may be painted with chalk dissolved in water.

Painting in two colors with large spots can be undertaken in two ways: one is to paint only part of the tank surface, leaving about 1/4 or 1/3 of the tank's surface in the original green; another is to repaint the tank entirely in two colors, either white and dark gray, or white and gray-brown.

When the weather is cold, painting should take place in a warm place, since paint applied when the temperature is 10° below zero Fahrenheit is too hard to be applied.

In winter, as in summer, it is necessary to avoid mechanical repetition of patterns and colors. For example, in painting the tanks of a platoon, one or two tanks are painted white, a third in white irregular stripes leaving parts of the protective green paint as it is, the fourth with white and dark gray spots, and finally, the fifth with white and grayish-brown spots.

c. Covers and Ground Masks

For winter tank camouflage, one may use nets made of cord which have fastened to them irregular white patches of fabric, about 1 yard across. A large all-white cover also may be used.

When using white winter covers, it is necessary to pay attention to the degree of whiteness of the materials used, for even if a little yellow shows or if part of the material is soiled, it will sharply outline the cover and the tank against the background of pure white snow. A simple method to improve this camouflage is to place a thin layer of snow on the cover.

In winter, ground masks are also used. But the construction of these camouflage masks involves special considerations dependent on the character of the background. The principal camouflage materials employed are irregularly shaped pieces of white fabric or painted white matting. In addition to the white patches, dark patches should be fastened to the material to give the appearance of bushes, tree tops, or other natural ground features. For dark patches one may use tree branches and other similar materials. As with covers, the use of white patches alone, or of a combination of white and dark patches, will depend entirely on the terrain and the coloration of the surroundings.

To attach the patches to the mask, they are frozen on after wetting the material with water.

d. Dummy Tanks

Drawing the attention of the enemy to dummy tanks has the same aim in wintertime as in summer, namely, to deceive the enemy concerning the disposition, types, and character of tank activity. However, in winter the making of dummy tanks is subject to certain special conditions. Large dummy snow tanks may be made by packing snow into the form of a tank, showing the hull, the suspension system, and the turret, and then spraying with paint. Movable life-size models are constructed not on wheels but on skis. "Flat" models may be made simply by treading the snow into the contours of a tank. In all other respects the making and use of dummy tanks in winter is no different than in summer.

e. Camouflage while in Motion

Generally speaking, winter conditions make it necessary to move along existing roads. Since winter roads appear to the aerial observer as dark strips, tanks which have an all-white winter paint stand out fairly clearly. In view of the fact that vehicles can be spotted by the shadow they cast, they should move on the side of the road nearest to the sun so that their shadow falls on the road, which is darker than the snow next to the road. Movement along the roads, especially at great speeds and over fluffy dry snow, gives itself away by clouds of snow dust. For this reason, movement of vehicles in wintertime should be at low speeds, especially over new-fallen snow. The tracks left by the tank treads stand out clearly as two dark parallel strips with tread impressions. These can be obliterated by sweeping the road. When tracks are left on the hard crust of the existing road it is necessary, instead of sweeping, to remove them with the aid of graders.

When the tanks pass through places where turns are unavoidable, there appear everywhere little heaps of upturned snow; these are characteristic marks and betray the movement of tanks. To prevent this, turns must be made gradually in a wide arc whenever practicable, or else the heaps of snow which are formed must be cleared away.

The reflection from the lenses of the tank headlights will also give away their movement. In order to prevent this, it is necessary to cover the headlights with white fabric covers, or some other material.

Finally, among the most important factors betraying the movement of tanks to ground observers is the clank of the tracks. [Russian tanks tracks are of all-metal construction.] The noise of these can be heard better as the temperature falls. Naturally, when operations are in the immediate vicinity of the enemy, one makes use not only of all the ordinary precautions employed in summer for the prevention of noise, but takes into account the special characteristics of winter weather with its increased transmission of sound.

f. Camouflage of Stationary Tanks

In winter, tanks are, generally speaking, parked alongside buildings and in woods and shrubbery; in exceptional cases it may be necessary to station tanks in open flat country or in gullies.

The peculiar characteristic of inhabited areas in wintertime from the point of view of camouflage is the motley appearance of the landscape due to the presence of dwelling places, barns, gardens, roads, and paths. This wealth and variety of outline affords considerable opportunities for concealing the position of tanks from air and ground observation by the enemy.

As a rule, all vehicles in bivouac should be placed under the roofs of sheds and barns. Only where there is an insufficient number of such structures, or where the size of the vehicles makes it impossible to place the vehicles in the existing shelters, is it necessary to build shelters, resembling the existing structures in the given locality. The roofs of these shelters must be covered with a layer of snow so that they will not look any different from the roofs of the existing structures. Just as in summertime, these camouflage structures may be built either as additions to existing structures or as separate structures. The separate camouflage structures should be situated along laid-out paths, and the tracks of the caterpillars which lead to the place where the tanks are stationed should be swept or dragged so as to resemble an ordinary road.

When there is not enough time to construct shelters, it is sometimes possible (as on the outskirts of a village) to camouflage tanks by simulating haystacks, piles of brushwood, stacks of building materials, etc. This is done by strewing over the vehicle a certain quantity of material at hand and covering it with a thin layer of snow.

Woods, orchards, and brushwood can be used for camouflage purposes in the wintertime only if additional camouflage precautions are taken. Since leafy woods offer much less concealment in winter than in summer and do not hide the vehicles from air observation, they must be covered with white covers, and there should be strewn over them broken branches or some other camouflage material such as hay, straw, etc.

When there are no white covers, the vehicles may be covered with dark ones, but snow must be placed on top and scattered. Dark covers can be used only against a background which has natural black spots. Finally, if no covers of any kind are available, the vehicles should be covered with branches, straw, hay, and the like, and snow placed on top in irregular patches.

When the tanks are stationed in open flat country, then the camouflage of the tanks also involves the breaking up of the uniform aspect of the locality, which is done by treading around on the snow. Then these areas are given irregular form by scattering here and there patches of pine needles, straw, and rubbish. The ground should also be laid bare, as tanks which are painted a dark color will not be easily discovered against a dark background, either by visual air observation or by the study of aerial photographs.

In open country, thaws are particularly favorable to camouflage of tanks, for the disappearing snow exposes portions of the surface of the ground. The result is that the ground assumes a naturally mottled appearance, and the contours of vehicles stationed there are easily blended. When there is deep snow, tanks may be placed in snow niches built near snowdrifts along the road. The entrances to these should be directly off the road in order to avoid tell-tale tracks of the treads. On the top the niches are covered with white covers, or with some other available material over which snow is placed. In order to camouflage the entrance, it is necessary to use hangings of white cloth or painted mats which may be readily let down or pulled up.

When the tank is stationed in a gully, it is covered with solid white covers of any kind of fabric or matting painted white, or by the regulation net, with white and black patches attached to it.

16. GERMAN DISCIPLINE

Tactical and Technical Trends,
No. 20, March 11th 1943

The short article translated below appeared in a Berlin daily newspaper dated April 8, 1942, and is believed to reflect the general attitude of the German civilian and military personnel toward the subject of discipline. This is the first article on this subject noted in the German press subsequent to the early summer of 1941. The controlled German press publishes news and articles written and edited to conform to the German viewpoint, as prescribed by the governing authorities. As can be seen from its text, this article appeals to the German's well-known pride in his discipline. The purpose of its publication was probably to console both the German soldier and civilian for hardships endured and for losses sustained during the severe winter in Russia in 1941-42. It was also intended to assist in maintaining the traditional high standard of discipline during the serious strain confronting the nation in the months to come. For these reasons, though not of recent publication, the article is felt to be pertinent at this time, in view of the present situation on the Russian Front.

The expression "military discipline" conveys a definite idea, which is inseparably linked with troop training. Discipline characterizes the appearance, behavior, performance, conduct, and value of military units.

An undisciplined company will execute an order haphazardly, or it will even fail to execute it at all. Without discipline, confusion reigns, and when the situation becomes serious under hostile fire, both coolness and cooperation are absent. Then the superior officer is no longer the actual commander.

There is a well-known saying: "Troops are like their commanders." Resolving this statement into the elements of discipline, it means that the commander must be the best-disciplined man in his unit if he demands obedience from each of his subordinates. It is an error to believe that military discipline consists only of obedience to the orders of officers and noncommissioned officers. True, this is ostensibly correct on the drill field or in a maneuver, but not in battle. In actual combat, there must be another kind of discipline, a self-discipline originating within the individual. This is differentiated from formal obedience chiefly by the fact that it prevails without the presence, the command, or the supervision of a superior; in addition, it is maintained under the stress of tense situations.

I recall the case of a sergeant who had been ordered to hold an advanced post under all circumstances. One morning, his post was cut off by the Soviets. His situation was hopeless. Nevertheless, he held his post in spite of heavy losses. He formed an island, an unassailable island, not so much in the tactical as in the moral sense. He held out, not because he knew that his comrades would come to his rescue, but because he possessed self-discipline which to him meant soldierly honor, decency, duty, and comradeship. His self-discipline forced him to stand and, if necessary, to fall at his post. It never entered his thoughts to question why it must be so. An order had been given, and naturally it would be executed.

The past winter has seen many such "islands" of the highest type of discipline. They have often ended in the sacrifice of life—the fulfillment of the last soldierly duty. They are the monuments to the great struggles occurring in recent months.

Soldierly discipline is not only a matter between superiors and subordinates; it involves outward actions as well as self-indoctrination. In order to stand the test, soldierly discipline requires: a firm foundation; a good military training, not too brief in duration; competent leadership; frequently a firm hand; exertions and privations; tests in courage under dangerous situations; information repeatedly as to what the battle is all about.

Military service demands a will to achieve the highest goal. It is not the individual action which decides, but rather a soldierly will on the part of each individual in the nation to carry out higher orders in a common effort. Therefore, in war, self-discipline is not restricted to the soldier alone. It is a matter that affects political, commercial, and cultural life as well as the life of the community and the family. It is the actual foundation of war, which is the fulfillment and demonstration of collective force. Self-discipline characterizes the individual as well as the entire nation. It is a matter of spirit, conscience, morals, and of the heart. It is the manifestation of a soldierly creed.

Comment:

In general, the German soldier, as well as the German civilian, considers discipline as a matter of honor. This trait in the German people is encouraged, developed, and exploited by their political as well as their military leaders, with a view to uniting all the German people in their war effort. This the leaders have succeeded in doing to a remarkable degree.

The German soldier, as a rule, takes pride in his ability to withstand hardships and privations. He frequently receives commendation from his officers and friends for his performance in this respect, but never effusive sympathy.

Keeping the soldier constantly informed as to why he is fighting, what the battle is about, and his part in it, has been found to pay dividends in improved discipline in combat.

It is believed that there is still a high standard of discipline in the German Army, maintained in spite of the hardships, privations, and losses incident to the present campaign in Russia.

17. OBSERVATIONS ON GERMAN EMPLOYMENT OF ARMORED INFANTRY

Tactical and Technical Trends, No. 22, April 8th 1943

The following account of the tactics of armored infantry was taken from a German training manual.

a. General

(1) Tanks

The rifle company transported in armored vehicles is a particularly strong unit in the attack because of its mobility, high fire power, and armor protection. The latter makes it possible to fight from the vehicles, but this is very rarely done. These units habitually dismount and fight on foot. The armor protection permits them to approach the enemy closely before dismounting. In view of its high allotment of heavy weapons, the company is able to carry out independent tasks.

Its main role is cooperation with tank units in carrying out the following tasks:

(a) Quick mopping-up and consolidation of ground overrun by the tanks;

(b) Supporting the tank attack by overcoming nests of enemy resistance, removing obstacles, and forming bridgeheads;

(c) Protection of assembly and bivouac areas.

b. Training

(1) Thorough training in fighting on foot must be given; at night, in all sorts of weather and all seasons, and over diversified terrain.

(2) All types of firing, especially at snap targets, must be practiced with both rifles and automatic arms, while the armored carrier is stationary and while it is in motion.

c. Fighting as Assault Troops

When the unit is used as assault troops, and also when fighting in woods, the weapons carried by the squads should be mostly submachine guns with plenty of HE and smoke grenades. Often only one machine gun will accompany the squad, but much extra ammunition will be distributed among several riflemen. The assault squads can borrow submachine gun, from the other squads. The heavy machine guns may go into action without their heavy mounts, but the mount should always be available. Mortars, from the vicinity of the carrier, coordinate their fire with that of the heavy machine guns.

d. The March

Over favorable terrain, an average speed of 15 mph can be maintained, with a maximum speed of from 18 1/2 to 22 1/2 mph under favorable conditions. This would permit a total of 90 to 120 miles per day. The interval between the point section and point platoon is about a minute, and between the point platoon and the company, 2 minutes. Antitank weapons, if carried, should be placed well forward, but other heavy weapons are normally placed in the rear. The company commander, and the commanders and observers of the artillery and heavy weapon units, usually travel behind the point platoon. Each platoon provides its own flank guards. Every 2 hours, a 20-minute halt should be made for minor repairs and refueling.

e. Fighting from the Carrier

The chief weapon in fighting from the carrier is the fixed (light) machine gun. Generally, this will be fired during halts of 15 to 25 seconds.

f. Attack in Cooperation with Tanks

The company will usually follow close behind the tanks to mop up points of resistance the tanks have by-passed. The leading troops will not dismount from their carrier, but will leave the fighting on foot to the succeeding waves. Antitank guns, if allotted, protect the flanks. Close contact will be maintained with the tanks ahead.

g. Pursuit

Close pursuit will be maintained, with every effort made to get behind and cut off the enemy, but when doing this, care must be taken to avoid being flanked in turn.

h. Defense
In defense, the armored infantry provides the outguard.

i. Retreat
Against an enemy on foot, withdrawal is made under cover of the armored infantry, which launches delaying counterattacks. Against an armored force, strong antitank fire must be provided, with constant reconnaissance on the flanks.

j. Battle under Special Conditions
(1) Attacking Strong Prepared Positions
The first two of the four carriers of an assault platoon drive forward through gaps in the minefields under cover of fire from the heavy weapons, directed at the casemates. They take position at the rear of the enemy defense areas. Against enemy tanks, smoke is used.

In the third carrier is the assault platoon leader, with squads detailed to hack through or blow out a lane in the wire. The fourth carrier, at 100 to 200 yards distance, follows up with ammunition and equipment.

(2) Fighting for Rivers
A swift attack to cut fuse connections will often prevent the enemy from blowing up bridges. If resistance is encountered, the patrols must report to the commanding officer, who may decide to cross elsewhere by means of rubber boats, or otherwise. Diversions should be practiced to draw the enemy away from the place of actual crossing. As soon as a crossing is made, the armored infantry will protect the bridgehead. Care must be used to prevent the dispersion of forces, and until a bridge is built, personnel carriers remain under cover from possible artillery fire.

(3) Fighting in Darkness or Fog
Careful preparation is necessary. In order to maintain direction the attack is usually made on foot along the lines of roads, streams, or ridges. Every effort is made to keep the carriers well forward, but

under cover, in case the fog lifts or daybreak comes.

(4) Fighting in Towns or Villages

As a rule, occupied towns are avoided. If necessary to attack them, setting fire to buildings will assist in making a breach in the defenses, and the attack is then pushed through courtyards and gardens rather than along streets.

(5) Fighting in Woods

Careful preparation and planning should be done when time permits. Where possible, the woods are split into sectors and cleared in detail. The thicker the woods, the closer must be the formations. Before crossing open spaces, close observation must be carried out. Cunning and surprise are often more profitable than prepared assault. At nightfall, the attack is broken off and the defense organized.

On the defensive, the position should be organized in depth well inside the edge of the woods. Trails are cleared and marked for rapid communication within the position. Listening posts near the edge of the woods keep the open country under observation; they are frequently relieved.

18. GERMAN WINTER FIELD FORTIFICATIONS, AND THE USE OF ICE-CONCRETE

Tactical and Technical Trends, No. 22, April 8th 1943

From the Eastern Front comes a report of the German type of winter field fortifications and shelters, with a description of an effective concrete made of a frozen sand, or sand with broken stone, and water mixture.

a. General

Construction of field fortifications in winter presents a number of special difficulties due to cold, frozen ground, ice, and snow which may occasionally reach a depth of several meters. The men's capacity for work is moreover lowered by extreme cold. For this reason allowance must be made for a considerable increase in time and personnel requirements, often amounting to many times the normal. Special tools and equipment suitable for work under winter conditions must be obtained well in advance.

The depth to which ground is frozen on the Eastern Front often reaches 1.5 meters (5 ft.).

b. Camouflage

In snow-covered terrain, special attention should be paid to concealment against ground and air observation. Paths caused by trampling, ditches, working sites, etc., can be recognized from the air with particular ease. For this reason, before beginning work snow should be cleared to one side so that it may be available for subsequent camouflage, and finished work must again be covered with snow. Trenches can be covered with planks, beams, pine branches, or sheet-iron, on which snow should be heaped.

c. Construction of Shelters, Trenches, and Breastworks

(1) Construction of Earth Shelters in Frozen Ground

(a) In the presence of the enemy, for speedy and silent preparation of shelters in frozen ground, sandbags are used; for this purpose, canvas rather than paper sacks are to be recommended. Sandbags are filled in the rear, and carried forward to the point where they are to be used. Freezing sandbags by pouring water on them improves their protective properties for the duration of cold weather.

(b) Where the tactical situation permits unimpeded work, the following practice is adopted. In constructing trenches in ground which is not frozen to a great depth, in order to avoid the labor of digging through the frozen ground, the surface is divided up by furrows into the desired sections. These sections are then undermined, and the frozen crust is caved in and removed. For this work heavy pickaxes, crowbars, iron wedges, etc., are necessary.

Deeply frozen ground can be broken up by engineers using power drilling equipment (concrete breakers driven by portable compressors) and explosives. Holes for explosives can be made in frozen ground by driving in red-hot, pointed iron rods or crowbars. In excavating trenches in deeply frozen ground, the best method is to dig holes at an interval of several feet down to the full depth of the trench; these holes are subsequently connected by tunnels under the frozen surface, and finally the surface is caved in.

(2) Construction of Shelters in Snow and Earth

If the depth of snow is great, fieldworks must be constructed partly in snow and partly in the ground. Small shafts are sunk to the full depth planned and are then connected by trenches dug in the snow. The deepening of these trenches into the ground can be carried out later. If there has been only a short frost before the snowfall, the ground will be found to be only slightly frozen, since the snow acts as a protective layer against hard freezing.

(3) Construction of Shelters in Snow

If heavy snowfall is to be expected, or if time is short, or if equipment for excavation of frozen ground is not available, breastworks of snow

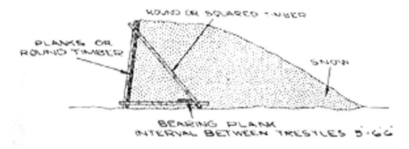

Figure 1

can be erected on the surface. Snow, if it is to be used as protection against enemy fire, must be tamped solid. It must also be camouflaged by scattering loose snow over it. Its effectiveness as a protection is raised by pouring water over it. The rear side of the breastwork should be revetted with sandbags filled with snow; canvas rather than paper should be used for this purpose. Alternative materials are round timber, wire netting, or wooden planks secured to posts, like a fence.

If it is impossible to drive in or anchor the posts, simple trestles of triangular cross section should be erected at intervals of 5 to 6 1/2 feet, as shown in figure 1. The best practice is to carry the trestles ready-made to the site where they are to be used. After adding the revetment and bearing planks, snow is shoveled over it and tamped hard. The center of the snow wall can be formed of any other suitable material: e.g., round timber, stones, gravel, sand, etc.

(4) Protective Qualities of Snow and Ice

The following are the thicknesses of snow and ice which afford

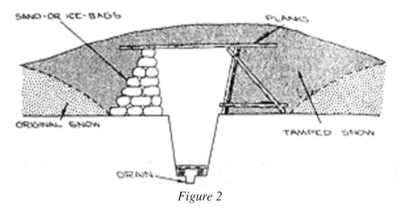

Figure 2

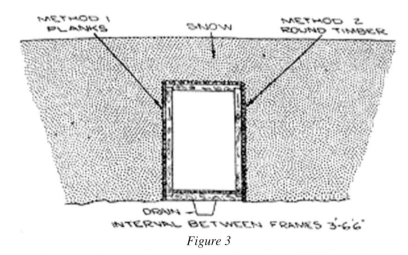

Figure 3

protection against ordinary rifle fire, but NOT against fire concentrated on a single point:

- New snow - (minimum) 13 ft
- Tamped snow - (minimum) 8 - 10 ft
- Frozen snow - (minimum) 6 ft 6 in
- Ice - (minimum) 3 ft 3 in

(5) Covered Trenches

Trenches can be covered over to protect them from snowing-up, and to conceal them, as shown in figure 2. The cover of round timbers, sawn timbers, planks, or beams must be strong enough to carry the maximum weight of snow that can be expected.

d. Tunneling in Snow

If the snow is sufficiently deep, tunnels can easily be constructed. They do not provide effective protection against artillery fire, but this disadvantage is considerably outweighed by the complete concealment they afford. The method of construction varies according to the condition of the snow, which may be new (powdery), already frozen, and of varying depths. The following are the methods employed:

(1) Digging in from the surface and covering over with planks and layers of snow;

(2) Digging in from the surface and the construction of sheeting or revetting with planks, beams, brushwood, or sheet-iron;

111

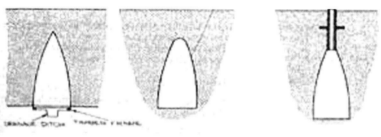

Figure 4   Figure 5

(3) Underground tunnelling, construction of wooden sheeting or revetting with planks, beams, or brushwood (figure 3);

(4) The construction of tunnels without sheeting (figure 4). In long tunnels, ventilation must be provided by ventilation shafts, as shown in figure 5.

e. Construction of Shelters, Covered Positions, Positions for AT or Infantry Guns, and Ammunition or Supply Shelters

The same methods are used as in construction in the ground. The floor and walls should be constructed with particular care, and the roofing formed of planks or beams. In addition, roofs and walls must be covered with roofing felt, which should also be laid under the floor. Inner insulation must also be provided by mats and straw, layers of wool, or sacking, and cracks should be filled with moss, sod, or straw. Another effective method of building walls is to use a double revetment of planks with a heat-insulating space between them. The revetment of intermediate space is necessary not only as protection against cold, but also to avoid the melting of the snow by internal heating stoves, etc. Doors and entrances should be small and well fitting. Even if shelters are unheated, a snow covering of sufficient thickness will raise the temperature in shelters of this kind to 3 to 5° C (37 to 41° F). Owing to their slight insulating properties, sheet-iron side walls are suitable only for excavations which are not to be occupied by personnel.

f. Drainage

When a thaw sets in, special provision must be made for draining away water, and this should be provided, when the position is first constructed, by ditches and other methods. Crawl-trenches and tunnels must be built with a gradient sufficient to drain the water away. Failure to observe these precautions will quickly result in the flooding of the excavation and the caving-in of the weakened and undercut walls.

g. "Ice-Concrete"

(1) Definition

Ice-concrete is a dense, frozen mixture of sand and water, or sand with gravel or broken stone and water.

(2) Application

Ice-concrete is especially suitable for reinforcement of breastworks and for the construction of roofs and shelters. An example is shown in figure 6 on the following page. Ice-concrete can be protected for a considerable period against effects of rising temperature by being covered with earth.

(3) Strength and Composition

Ice-concrete is many times stronger than normal ice. Regarding its composition, experience is as follows:

(a) A high proportion of fine sand increases the strength. The strongest mixture of all is composed of sand alone.

(b) If insufficient sand is available, gravel or broken stone can be used. The proportion of fine sand should, however, not fall below 10 percent.

(c) A small proportion of topsoil, clay, or mud is not injurious.

(d) Only as much water should be added as the mixture is capable of absorbing, and as will cause it to become slightly liquid.

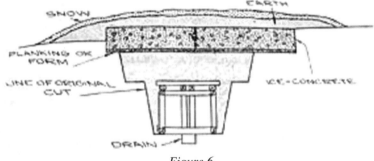

Figure 6

(4) Preparation of Ice-Concrete

(a) In preparing the mixture by hand, it is shovelled over, if possible in a trough, and the water added gradually; or, mixing can be done in a concrete mixer. The wet mixture is immediately poured into the forms. This operation is carried out in layers of from 4 to 6 inches, accompanied by tamping, in order to consolidate the mixture.

If gravel is used, the material is pre-mixed without adding water. The mixture is then poured into the forms in layers 4 to 6 inches thick, and water is poured in to complete saturation, accompanied by stirring and tamping.

(b) In both cases successive layers should be added as soon as the previous layer is beginning to freeze. Freezing takes place more slowly if the water is added later. In order to hasten the process of freezing, sand and gravel should be already at a freezing temperature before water is added, and the water itself should be as cold as possible. If the material is frozen in large lumps, it should be broken up before mixing.

(c) Ordinary wooden forms should be used, but snow, ice, earth, straw, or brushwood can also be used for this purpose.

As a protection against warming from inside (i.e., heating by stoves, etc.), the inner forms are left standing. The outer forms should be removed as soon as possible in order to hasten freezing.

As a guide, it may be noted that a sheet of ice-concrete, 4 inches thick, will be completely frozen at a temperature of 13 degrees below zero, F°, in 4 to 6 hours.

19. GERMAN VIEWS ON RUSSIAN SUMMER CAMOUFLAGE

Tactical and Technical Trends,
No. 23, April 22nd 1943

The following is a translation of a German pamphlet on Russian summer camouflage, printed in the spring following the German invasion of Russia in June 1941. The Germans evidently found Russian camouflage methods disconcerting, and some were apparently new to them. The great care the Russians apparently devote to camouflage training is worthy of note; their success in effective concealment seems to have resulted from ingenuity and strict camouflage discipline.

a. Preface

The following examples are taken from reports from the front and captured orders. They represent only a part of Russian camouflage methods, but are in some cases new and worthy of imitation. They can be used in improvised form by our own troops. A detailed knowledge of Russian camouflage and methods helps our own troops to recognize the enemy and his tricks without delay. In this way surprise is avoided and troops can operate with greater confidence.

b. Camouflage Material

The camouflage instinct is strongly developed in the Russian, and his inventive ability is astounding. This gift is systematically encouraged by thorough camouflage training which begins on the first day of military training and is continued throughout the whole period. Camouflage discipline is good even among troops who otherwise might be well below the average as regards weapon training. Infringements of camouflage discipline are severely punished.

(1) Prepared Camouflage Material

(a) Summer Camouflage Suit

The suit consists of a jacket and hood of green-colored material in

Figure 1

which tufts of matting in various shades are woven. In appropriate surroundings, a man in a prone position in this clothing cannot be seen more than a few paces away.

(b) Summer Camouflage Smock

This consists of colored material with patches in dark shades, and is suitable for use with a broken background of woods and bushes.

(c) Camouflage Net for Rifleman

The net is about 5 by 2 1/2 feet and weighs about 1/3 pound. It is woven with natural camouflage material taken from the immediate surroundings and can be used either as a covering or spread out in front of the rifleman. By binding several nets together, rifle pits, machine guns, and entrances to dugouts can be camouflaged.

(d) Camouflage Mask for Rifleman

This consists of a wire contraption divided into several pieces, covered with material. In it is a hole through which the rifle can protrude. It represents a bush and is in use in three different colors. It can be folded up and carried on the person in a bag. The rifleman lies in such a position behind the mask that his body is fully hidden. In attacking he can move forward in a crouch and push the mask in front of him. The mask is only visible to the naked eye at a distance of 150 to 200 paces.

(e) Camouflage Cover for Machine Gun

The cover consists of colored fabric in which tufts of colored matting are woven. When moving forward, the cover will not be taken off. The machine gun with this cover can only be recognized when within about 100 yards.

(f) Camouflage Fringe

The fringe consists of a band about 3 yards long, from which grass colored matting is hung. On the ends are hooks for attaching the fringe on the object. The rifleman can fix the fringe on the helmet or shoulders. Five of these fringes are used to camouflage a machine gun, and six for an antitank gun.

(g) Nets

For covering gun positions and trenches, nets of various sizes are issued. The net is woven with shreds of matting or paper; when in use, additional natural camouflage is added, such as grass, twigs, etc. These nets are also used by tanks, tractors, trucks, and trailers. The standard net is about 12 feet square, and by joining several together, large surfaces can be camouflaged against aerial observation (see figure 1).

(h) Camouflage Carpet

This consists of shreds of various sizes into which colored matting and tufts are woven. It is used mostly for camouflaging earth works.

(2) Improvised Camouflage Material

(a) Observation and Sniper Posts

A tree stump is hollowed out and stakes are used as supports. Another method is to insert periscopes into a frame made to look like wooden crosses in cemeteries (see figure 2 overleaf). Imitation hayricks are often used.

Figure 2

Figure 3

Figure 4

(b) Camouflage Against Observation from the Air

Shadows can be cast by fixing frameworks on the side of a house or on the roof so that the object cannot be recognized. Branches fixed on wire strung over the object can make it invisible from the air (see figure 3).

(c) Camouflaging Tanks and Tank Tracks

Tanks when being transported by rail or when on the road can be made to look like roofed freight cars or ordinary trucks.

When there are groups of trees, camouflage can be quickly obtained by bending the tops of the branches over the objects to be camouflaged (see figure 4). Nets can also be spread over and attached to the trees, with natural material laid on top. Among low bushes, tanks can be covered with grass, moss, or twigs. Freshly cut trees, one-and-a-half times the height of the object to be camouflaged, complete the camouflage. Tanks on a slope can be effectively and quickly camouflaged by the use of netting or other covers. Tanks in hollows can be made invisible by covers and, even without natural camouflage, nets or covers can completely alter the shape of tanks.

Tank tracks can be obliterated by dragging a fir tree behind the tank; rolls of barbed wire with an iron rod through them can also be used for this purpose.

c. Use of Camouflage

(1) On the March

As equipment being transported by rail cannot be fully concealed, the Russians attach particular importance to preventing the recognition of the type of equipment by making guns, vehicles, tanks, fuel trucks, etc., look like ordinary roofed freight cars. This is done by means of some sort of superstructure. Loading and unloading generally take place at night, often in open country.

Movement of large Russian units takes place either at night, with meticulous attention being paid to blackout regulations, or by day in wooded country. If the march must take place by day in country which offers only limited natural concealment, movement takes place by bounds from cover to cover. Motor vehicles are, where possible, diverted from main roads to side or wood roads. All bunching of vehicles on bridges, defiles, etc., is strictly avoided. A group of vehicles will halt under cover a distance from a defile; the movement through the defile will be made only by single vehicles or in small groups.

On the approach of German aircraft, vehicles of all descriptions take cover without delay. If single vehicles are forced to remain on the road, they either remain stationary, or, failing any camouflage protection, they take up positions diagonally on the road in order to look like broken-down vehicles.

Track discipline is carefully carried out. When tanks have to leave the main road, they travel in single column as far as possible so as not to give away their numbers by leaving many tracks.

(2) Quarters and Bivouacs

All evidence of the occupation of a village is avoided. Tanks, guns, and vehicles, if they cannot be brought under cover, are placed in irregular formations and camouflaged in yards and gardens, and against hedges, bushes, walls, and trees.

Special care is taken to see that movement from one place to another is limited to small groups; this rule applies also when issuing food, gasoline, etc.

Destroyed villages and burned-down premises are preferred for quartering men, weapons, equipment, and vehicles, as these areas lend themselves easily to camouflage.

Bivouacs are cleverly camouflaged against houses, hedges, gardens, etc. If possible, thick woods are used, and use is made of branches. In open country, hollows and ditches are used to the utmost, and bivouacs spread out in irregular formations. Tents are covered with natural camouflage material; if this is lacking, no use is made of tents. Instead, holes and pits are constructed. When bivouacs are taken up, tracks are obliterated in order to give the enemy no indication as to strength.

(3) Battle

Stress is laid on the necessity of being able to crawl for long distances at a quick pace. Patrols are well equipped with camouflage suits, and make full use of darkness and bad visibility.

When working forward, the Russian moves in short, quick bounds, and is capable of moving through the thickest undergrowth in order to work his way close to the enemy position. If the defense is on the alert, he is able to lie still for hours on end.

Russian tree snipers are particularly difficult to recognize. Tank-destroying sections with Molotov cocktails, grenades, and mines, are distributed in wheat fields and at places several yards from the edges of woods and fields.

In defending built-up areas, the Russians make use of positions outside the area. These consist of many rifle pits, organized in depth and well camouflaged with fences and bushes. When firing from houses, machine guns are placed well back from windows and doorways to prevent the flash being seen, and also to smother the report.

When German aircraft appear, every movement ceases.

After firing, any discoloration in front of a gun is covered with suitable camouflage material. When the gun remains for some time

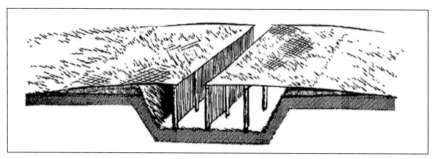

Figure 5

in one position, a board of sufficient size, and colored to match the surroundings, can be laid in front of the muzzle.

As the presence of tanks leads to definite conclusions regarding the main effort of the attack, the Russians are very careful to camouflage their armor.

(4) Layout of Defense Positions

Reconnaissance patrols are instructed not only to study the ground from the tactical point of view but also as regards possibilities for camouflage. This includes shape of the ground formations, the background, the coloring, the available natural camouflage, and what suitable artificial camouflage material can be used. Positions are selected to conform to the natural contours of the ground, and comfort is of secondary importance. As much use as possible is made of reverse slope positions. Parapets are kept as low as possible and are carefully camouflaged with grass, etc. Positions are often camouflaged with covers made of boards, fir branches, or straw. If time does not allow, only single portions of the trench system will be covered, so that to an observer they look like connecting trenches. Provision is made to conceal vision slits. Antitank ditches are either entirely covered, or partially covered in such a way that they look like narrow, easily passable ditches (see figure 5). Pillboxes are carefully camouflaged with nets or covers. The open walls are painted with a mixture of tar and asphalt, and covered with earth or hay. Wire obstacles can be made invisible by passing them through hedges and fences.

In woods, thick undergrowth is preferred in selecting a position.

Cutting down trees to give fields of fire is avoided for reasons of camouflage.

Russian signalmen use telegraph poles, with the bark still on, and set them up at irregular distances. The line of poles is laid to conform with the country. Earth at the foot of the poles is carefully camouflaged, and trampling of the earth along the line of the poles is strictly avoided. Wire is also laid to conform with the general contouring.

Camouflage discipline in occupied positions is very good, and one seldom hears talking, rattling of weapons, or sees the glimmer of a cigarette. In order to prevent the enemy realizing that a position is weakly held, single riflemen keep up strong fire activity at various points.

d. Dummy Positions

The Russians often use dummy positions.

Dummy trenches are of normal width, but are dug only to a depth of about 1 1/2 feet. The bottom can be made dark with soot or pine needles. Dummy dugouts can be made by the use of props, with the entrance made of cardboard or paper. Dummy loopholes and observation slits can be made out of black paper or felt. Dummy gun positions can be arranged by turning over grass, or burning it in order to imitate discoloration from muzzle blast. Dummy gun positions must be at correct distances. The representation of dummy tracks leading to the dummy positions must not be forgotten. The desired result is achieved by mowing grass to the normal width of a track, and letting the mown grass remain, or rolling it. When the ground is open, color must be used in order to make the tracks light and trenches dark.

Dummy obstacles can be erected by mowing grass and making little heaps out of the cut grass. On a ploughed field, it is sufficient to plough at right angles to the furrows to the width of the particular obstacle it is desired to represent. Dummy mine pits can be made by taking out sods of turf and laying them down clumsily. The dummy minefields should be two to four times as obvious as the normal. In dummy minefields 5 to 10 percent of live mines are generally laid. Dummy light installations are used a great deal in order to portray a station, industrial plant, or airfield. Lanterns, dummy bivouacs, and camp fires are often arranged to give the impression of the presence of troops.

20. SOME GERMAN BATTLE OBSERVATIONS ON THE RUSSIAN FRONT

Tactical and Technical Trends, No. 23, April 22nd 1943

Below appears a translation of a German document discussing in outline form one of their later Russian offensives.

a. Preparation

Detailed preparation for the attacks was made possible through the constant collection of information dealing with previous actions, exchange of information between various headquarters and distribution of this information down to companies. Preparations included rehearsals over similar ground and under similar conditions; also, measures to deceive the enemy.

b. The Attack

The attack was carried out by surprise, with no artillery registration or preparation. The attack opened with coordinated fire on a narrow front from artillery and all smoke mortars and heavy weapons available. As success depends upon speedy removal of obstacles in depth, especially minefields, strong engineer elements were allotted to the leading elements. Cooperation with the air force was close. Flight schedules were arranged to leave sufficient time for refueling and resupply of ammunition. To avoid bombing of friendly troops, the air force was kept closely informed of the positions of troops on the ground by the aid of air-force liaison officers, and by ample supplies of cloth panels, etc.

c. Minefields

Minefields were quickly crossed by reconnaissance and by mine-detector sections, pushed well forward to mark the lanes. Mine-clearing sections rapidly widened the lanes through the fields from 5 to 10 meters. Two lanes were made for each company sector.

d. Observations

(1) Whenever strong tank attacks were launched, the Russians coordinated the fire of all available antitank guns, and antiaircraft guns in an antitank capacity.

(2) The Russians would often let our attack come so close that our artillery could not continue to fire. Heavy weapons were therefore pushed well forward for use against positions where such tactics were expected.

(3) Mass formations had to be avoided in favor of organization in depth.

(4) When signal communications had not been set up, traffic difficulties were encountered between responsible headquarters.

The use of the Fieseler Storch (a small liaison and command plane capable of landing and taking off in a very small space) was necessary for commands responsible for observing battle situation and directing traffic.

21. GERMAN VIEWS ON RUSSIAN TACTICS IN WOODS

Tactical and Technical Trends, No. 23, April 22nd 1943

Much thought has been devoted to the tactics employed by the Japanese in the close jungle country of the southwest Pacific areas. Of particular interest therefore is the following brief extract from a German training pamphlet.

The terrain of the Eastern Front and Russian methods of fighting are both such that battles have often to be fought in thick, marshy, and extensive woods. To overcome their nervousness of woods, officers and men must be trained in forest fighting, a training which serves equally as training for fighting by night or in fog.

The following is an account of some lessons learned in fighting on the Russian Front.

When fighting in woody or marshy terrain, the Russians show their greatest powers of resistance. Here, their superiority of numbers, cunning and skill at camouflage stand them in good stead. They are adept in the use of ground, in the use of trees for observation and as sniping posts, and at erecting field fortifications in woods. They deliberately seek out woods for purposes of approach and defense; by holding their fire, they entice the enemy to approach within a short distance and come to grips in close-quarter fighting. Despite the thickness of the undergrowth and the density of the trees, they even strengthen their defense with tanks, and attack against them then becomes difficult and costly.

The Russians tend to make great use of the edges of woods, and in particular to concentrate heavy weapons and antitank guns at points where trails and roads enter the woods. The Russians do not surrender even when the woods may be surrounded. They must, therefore, be attacked and destroyed within the woods.

Lines of communication which run through woods, even when

they may be behind the front, are particularly precarious. When they retreat, the Russians leave detachments behind in woods. These detachments, reinforced possibly by others dropped from planes, form partisan bands for the special task of harassing the enemy and of interfering with his rear communications. The mopping up of woods which may have been occupied by partisan or other dispersed groups of Russians demands much time and the planned use of sufficient forces. Merely to comb out roads that may run through woods is fruitless and costly, for the Russians disperse off the roads into the woods.

22. GERMAN CLOSE-IN TACTICS AGAINST ARMORED VEHICLES

Tactical and Technical Trends,
No. 23, April 22nd 1943

The following is a translation of a German document issued early in 1942. While some of the methods of attack discussed may have since been altered, it is thought that it reflects the essentials of current German doctrine. The preface explains the scope and purpose of the document.

Current Instructions For Close-in Tactics Against Armored Vehicles

Preface

These directives are based on experiences of the German Army in close-in combat against Russian tanks on the Eastern Front. The Russian tactics so far as known have been taken into consideration.

New doctrines of our own are in process of development and will be available to the troops after completion, together with directions as to their use. First, the Eastern Army will be equipped with incendiary bottles. Presumably the troops at the front use means of fighting about which, at the time of publication of these directives, no description is yet at hand. In addition, new enemy methods will appear, which will be adapted to our own fighting.

These directives, therefore, present only preliminary instructions. Cooperation of the troops in the field is needed for their completion. To this end, new fighting practices of our own and of the enemy should be reported, with drawings and descriptions of battle conditions at the time. Communications should be sent through the service channels to the General of Infantry and to the General of Mobile Troops in the Army High Command.

The importance of close-in fighting against tanks makes it imperative that individual tank hunters be trained immediately in all the arms. The state of training in the Reserve Army will be tested by recruit inspections.

These directives apply to combat against all kinds of armored vehicles. For simplification, only tanks are mentioned in the text.

I. General

1. If there are no armor-piercing weapons at hand, or if their fire does not show sufficient result against attacking tank forces, specially trained, organized, and equipped tank hunters will have to assault and destroy tanks by close-in combat, making use of their special assault weapons and without waiting for specific orders. All other available arms will lend their support as strongly as possible.

Experience proves that with proper training and skilled use of close-in weapons, all classes of tanks can be destroyed by individual soldiers.

2. Close-in combat against tanks demands courage, agility, and a capacity for quick decision, coupled with self-discipline and self-confidence. Without these qualities, the best combat weapons are of no use. Proper selection of personnel is therefore of decisive importance.

3. Thorough knowledge of enemy tank types and of their peculiarities and weaknesses in battle and movement, as well as complete familiarity with the power and use of our own weapons in every terrain, is necessary for successful combat. This will strengthen the self-confidence of the troops. It will also make up the crucial points in training.

4. Close-in combat against tanks may be necessary for all situations and all troops.

In the first place the combat engineers, and tank hunters are the mainstays of this type of fighting. It must be demanded that each member of these arms master the principles and weapons of close-in antitank combat, and that he use them even when he does not belong to an antitank squad.

5. Over and above this, soldiers of all the armed services should be selected and grouped into close-in tank-hunting squads consisting

of one leader and at least three men. They must continually be ready for close-in combat with tanks.

Where special close-in weapons are not at hand, expedients should be devised.

Combining tank-hunting squads into tank-hunting groups may be useful under certain conditions.

6. The equipment for close-in tank hunting consists of the following: incendiary bottles and Tellermines, TNT, automatic weapons (our own or captured), submachine guns, Very pistols, hand grenades, smoke bottles, and camouflage material, as well as hatchets, crowbars, etc., to use as clubs for the bending of machine-gun barrels projecting from the tank. Of this equipment the useful and available weapons for blinding, stopping, and destroying the tank should always be carried along. In the interest of maximum mobility, the tank-hunting soldiers must be free of all unnecessary articles of equipment.

II. Combat Principles

7. Careful observations of the entire field of battle, early warning against tanks, as well as continuous supply and readiness of tank-hunting equipment of all kinds and in ample quantity, will insure against surprise by enemy tanks and will permit their swift engagement.

8. It should be standard procedure continually to observe the movements and the action of tank-hunting squads and to support them by the combined fire of all available weapons. In this connection, armor-piercing weapons must direct their fire on the tanks while the remaining weapons will fight primarily against infantry accompanying the tanks. It will be their mission to separate the infantry from the tanks.

Sometimes tanks carry infantrymen riding on them, who protect the tanks at forced or voluntary halts against the attack of tank hunters. These security troops must be destroyed by supporting infantry before the tank hunters attempt to assault the vehicles. Should the tanks arrive without infantry, the fire of all the available weapons will be concentrated against the vulnerable places of the tank. The shorter the range and the more massed and heavy the fire, the greater the physical and moral effect.

Fire by sharpshooters is always of special value.

The activity of tank-hunting squads should not be hampered by the supporting fire. The mission of such supporting fire is to split up tank forces, to blind and put the crews out of action, and to have a demoralizing effect on them, thereby creating favorable conditions for close-in assault.

In case fire support by other weapons is impossible, the attack by tank-hunting squads must proceed without it.

9. The basic principles of close-in assault are the same in all battle situations. In defense, knowledge of the terrain and of the time available will be profitable for the preparation and the attack.

10. The carrying out of close-in combat will largely depend on the immediate situation. The number, type, and tactics of the attacking tank force, the terrain, our own position, and the effect of our own defensive fire will always vary, and this variation will demand great adaptability and maneuverability on the part of our tank hunters.

11. Only one tank can be assaulted by a tank-hunting squad at one time. If several tanks attack together and if only one tank-hunting squad is available, then that tank is to be assaulted which at the moment appears as the most dangerous or whose engagement promises the quickest success. In general, the choice must be left to the tank-hunting squad.

If there is a sufficient number of squads available, it is advisable, particularly in defense, to hold one or more squads ready in the rear for the destruction of tanks which may break through.

12. Generally speaking, the procedure will always be: first, to blind the tank, then to stop it, and finally to destroy the vehicle and the crew in close-in combat.

13. Whether the tank-hunting squads advance at the beginning of a tank attack or whether they leave their foxholes only during the engagement or whether the whole assault goes on from under cover depends entirely on the situation.

The behavior of the squads depends on whether the tank is moving or is voluntarily or involuntarily halted.

The attack on a heavy or super-heavy tank will often be easier than on a light tank, because the former in general is clumsier and has poorer observation. But the destruction of heavy tanks generally demands the use of more powerful weapons.

14. It is important in every case to make full use of the dead space around each tank.

In general, tanks should be attacked from the side or the rear. Any moment of weakness of the enemy tank should be utilized (i.e., impeded vision, halts, climbing and overcoming of obstacles, etc.).

15. Tanks should be approached by crawling and stalking, making full use of cover and concealment.

16. The foxholes of tank hunters must be narrow and have steep walls. They must be built without parapets and must not be recognizable by enemy tanks. They may be camouflaged either by canvas strips or branches. Whenever possible they should be protected by a belt of mines.

17. The tank hunters will remain motionless in their foxholes observing their targets and waiting in readiness for the favorable moment to assault. They must face the enemy tank calmly and must have the nerve to "let it come." It is always wrong to run away. While moving, the single soldier is inferior to the tank. In hiding, on the contrary, he is usually superior. He is safest inside the dead area around the enemy tank.

In villages, close-in assault of tanks is usually easier than in open terrain because of the abundant possibilities for hiding and cover (as by roof-snipers).

Often the corner of a house, a bush, or a fence are sufficient as hiding places.

By the use of obstacles of all kinds, dummy mines and guns, and signs like "Warning — mines!", enemy tanks may be guided into terrain unfavorable to them, but favorable for the assault squads and antitank weapons.

18. When attacking moving tanks, the tank hunters at first must be well concealed and permit the tank to come close to them (7 to 20

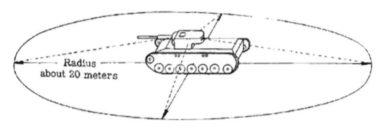

Figure 1

meters); then they try to stop the tank by blinding it, or at least they force it to slow down. A strong blinding effect is obtained through the massed fire of all weapons. By using explosive charges, tank hunters destroy the tracks of the tank and cripple it. They will then assault it and destroy it and its crew with their close-in weapons.

In the case of halted tanks, the squad stalks up on it using the terrain to its best advantage.

19. Around every tank there is a dead area which it cannot cover with its principal weapons. The higher a tank, the larger, usually, is its dead space. In general, this space has a radius of about 20 meters (see figure 1). To combat targets in the dead space, tanks have slits through which pistols and submachine guns can be fired. Frequently a machine gun is found on the rear side of the turret.

When assaulting a tank, the tank hunters must make use of the dead space. They should approach the tank from the direction which is opposite to the direction of its principal weapons. This is also opposite to the direction of its principal observation (see figure 2). Should this approach be impracticable because of a machine gun in

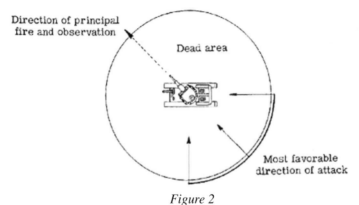

Figure 2

the back of the turret, the squad will attack from the side or diagonally from the rear.

20. The tank hunter with the principal close-in weapon will use it against the tank while the other tank hunters support him with their fire. Should he be impeded by that fire, it must cease. When the crew of the tank becomes aware of the assault, they will open the turret hatch so as to defend themselves with hand grenades. That instant will be used by the observing tank hunters to fire against the open turret and to wound the crew. Crews of stalled or burning tanks who do not give themselves up when getting out will be destroyed in close combat. If the tanks are still undamaged, they are made useless by removal of the breech-blocks, by destroying the machine guns, and by setting fire to the gasoline tanks.

21. Neighboring units support the attack by rifle and machine-gun fire against the vision slits of the attacking tanks as well as against accompanying infantry which might endanger the tank hunters. The tanks are blinded and prevented from taking accurate aim, and the enemy infantry is forced to take cover. Weak places of the tank are taken under fire with armor-piercing ammunition and antitank weapons. Lead-sprays entering through the shutters into the inside of the tank will wound the crew. The cooperation of the tank-hunting squads with other troops in the area must be previously arranged, and all signals decided upon.

III. Close-in Combat Weapons and Their Use

22. There are several kinds of short-range media (blinding, burning, and explosive) which allow many variations of use. The type of armored vehicle, its position, and the terrain determine which of the available weapons are to be used, or if several should be combined. The leader of the tank-hunting squad will have to decide quickly which medium to adopt under the circumstances.

According to the doctrine "Blind, halt, destroy," the tank-hunting squad has to be equipped with blinding, explosive, and incendiary materials. Explosives have the double purpose of stopping and destroying the tanks.

Blinding Agents

Smoke Candles and Smoke Grenades

23. Smoke candles or several smoke hand grenades, thrown in front of the tank with allowance for wind direction, minimize its vision and force it to slow up.

Smoke

24. Common smoke is used like smoke from candles. To be able to obtain it at the right moment, distribute straw or other highly inflammable material in the probable avenue of approach, drench it with gasoline or kerosene, and ignite it with signal rockets at the approach of tanks.

The detonation of grenades and artillery shells also creates clouds of smoke. Moreover, the firing of armor-piercing grenades against the vision slits promises success.

25. When smoke is used, the tanks are hidden also to our antimechanized weapons, and they are unable to aim accurately. Therefore, smoke should be used only when the vehicles have come so near that they cannot be covered by fire any longer without endangering our own troops, and therefore have to be destroyed at close range.

Signal Rockets

26. Signal rockets shot against vision slits have a blinding effect,

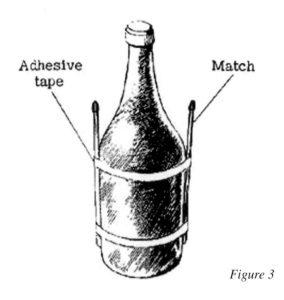

Adhesive tape   Match

Figure 3

particularly at dusk and in the dark; also, the vehicle is illuminated for our antitank weapons. Note that signal rockets only begin to burn at a distance of 25 meters.

Covering of Vision Slits

27. For this purpose one man jumps onto the tank, preferably from the rear, or approaches the tank closely from the side, and covers the vision slits or periscopes with a blanket, overcoat, shelter half, etc., or applies mud, paint, or grease. This is possible only if the tank is moving slowly or is halted, and if it is not protected by the fire from other tanks or following infantry. Any tank crew will be strongly demoralized by the presence of an enemy on top of their tank.

Incendiary Agents

Flame-throwers

28. Flame-throwers are aimed at vision slits, weapon openings, ventilators, and engine cover.

Incendiary Bottles

29. Incendiary bottles are a combat weapon used against tanks, armored scout cars, and other cars. In street and house fighting, they can also be used against living targets. They are thrown against the front part of the tank for blinding purposes, over the engine for incendiary purposes.

The contents of an incendiary bottle (not self-igniting) are 2/3 gasoline and 1/3 fuel oil. Ignition of the incendiary bottles takes place (when it has broken after hitting a hard surface) by the use of special safety matches.

The incendiary bottles are packed in wooden boxes in damp sawdust. The boxes also contain adhesive tape for fastening the matches to the bottles. The safety matches are packed in batches of twenty with 3 scratch pads in containers of noninflammable material. Two safety matches are taped to the bottle. The heads of the safety matches can be pointed either toward the neck or to the bottom of the bottle (see figure 3). The matches are lighted immediately before throwing the incendiary bottle, by friction with any rough surface or the match box. See that both matches are burning properly.

The bottles can be thrown in two different ways; throwing by

Figure 4

swinging the arm, holding the bottle at the neck (see figure 4), or throwing by pitching, like putting a shot, grasping the bottle at its heaviest point (see figure 5).

Either of the two ways is practicable. In general, the position of the thrower will determine the type of throw. In a prone or similar position he will not be able to swing his arm, and therefore will have to pitch it. Whenever possible it should be thrown like a stick hand grenade, because the accuracy of aim is greater and the possible range will be increased.

The most vulnerable parts of a tank are: the engine (ventilation — on tanks usually in the rear), the vision slits, and imperfectly closed hatches.

Should an incendiary bottle miss and remain intact, it is better to leave it until the matches have burned out, as the heightened pressure might cause an explosion. The bottles should be handled with care. They should not be bumped together or against hard objects.

Improvised Incendiary Bottles

30. Any bottle can be filled with an inflammable liquid, preferably mixed with wool fiber, cotton, or torn rags. A good mixture is two-thirds gasoline and one-third oil. Note that Flame-oil #19 is not

Figure 5

freeze-proof. A mixture of gas and fuel oil can be used instead.

To ignite it, the bottle is equipped with an improvised lighter. It is constructed in the following way:

A wick is passed through a hole in the cork of the bottle, so that one end hangs in the liquid. To the free end are attached several matches. Several wicks may also be used without the cork, if they completely close the opening of the bottle and are well drenched in the fluid (see figure 6).

At the approach of the tank, the wick is lighted and the bottle thrown. When it breaks, the fluid is ignited by the wick and is distributed over the tank and its engine. Generally the tank catches

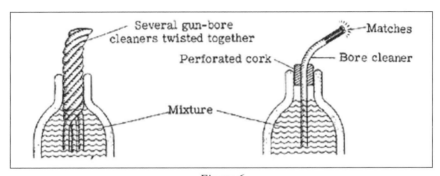

Figure 6

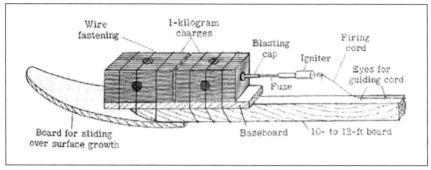

Figure 7

fire. If further bottles are thrown against the tank, they do not have to be ignited before throwing. Even initially a bottle without an ignition device can be used. After breaking the bottle on the tank, the liquid can be ignited with signal rockets, hand grenades, smoke candles, smoke grenades, burning torches, or burning gasoline-drenched rags.

Captured Enemy Incendiary Bottles

Bottles with a self-igniting phosphorus mixture (so-called Molotov cocktails) are used as explained in paragraphs 29 and 30. If large numbers of these weapons are captured, they should be collected and reported, to enable distribution among as many troops as possible.

Gasoline

32. Several quarts of gasoline are poured over the engine housing of the tank, and ignited as in paragraph 30. Gasoline can also be poured into a tank. It is then ignited by a hand grenade which is also pushed in.

Hand Grenades

33. Quite frequently an enemy is forced to open the hatch for better observation. This opportunity can be used to throw grenades in a high arc into the interior of the tank. The crew can thus be eliminated and the tank set afire. Sometimes it may be possible to open the hatches with crow bars or bayonets and throw grenades into the interior.

Smoke Candle or Smoke Grenade

34. When thrown (as in paragraph 33) into the interior of the tank, they start the tank burning, or at least force the crew to get out because of the thick smoke.

Signal Rockets

35. Signal rockets shot into open hatches with a Very pistol can also start a tank burning.

Explosives

Hand Grenades

36. Several hand grenades can be combined into one concentrated charge (see paragraph 38).

One-Kilogram Blasting Slab

37. A slab of 1 kilogram *[2.2 pounds]* of explosive, placed on top of a tank, has about the same strength as a concentrated charge of 7 hand grenades and gives the crew a severe shock. Two such concentrated charges damage the turret hatch considerably and for a short time make the crew unable to fight because of the high concussion. Two or three such charges combined into a multiple charge can so severely damage the tracks of tanks that they will soon break under use. Even better are two such concentrated charges combined into an elongated charge. For this purpose, two to three 1-kilogram charges are tied to a board with wire and equipped with a short piece of fuze (see figure 7).

To destroy machine-gun and cannon barrels protruding from the tank, two 1-kilogram charges are tied together, hung like a saddle over the top of the barrel, and detonated (see figure 8). Machine-gun barrels are torn by the explosion, and cannon barrels bent sufficiently so that an attempt to fire the gun will completely destroy it. Inserting hand grenades into the muzzle of the guns also has good results against cannon and crew. Shells will also burst in the barrel if stones,

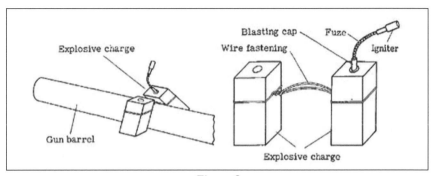

Figure 8

wood, or earth are rammed into it. Placing hand grenades in the vision slits is also effective.

Several 1-kilogram charges can be tied together as a field expedient in case of lack of finished multiple charges.

Concentrated Charges

38. The bodies of seven stick grenades are tied together securely with wire so that they will not fall apart when used. Only the middle grenade is fitted with the usual handle with an internal igniter (see figure 9). This charge is ineffective against the armor or tracks of heavy tanks. But the concussion of the charge, exploded on top of the tank, will be so strong that the crew will be knocked out temporarily.

39. The concentrated charge of 3 kilograms, is found ready for use in the infantry engineer platoon, infantry engineer platoon motorized, engineer companies, and engineer battalions.

It will pierce about 60 mm of armor and is best placed over the engine or the driver's seat. The crew will be badly wounded by small fragments of the inner walls spattering off. The concussion is unbearable. To destroy the tracks, the charge must fully be covered by them.

Even greater effect will be obtained by combining several 3-

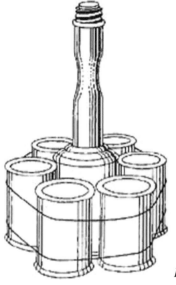

Figure 9

Figure 10

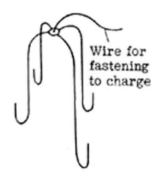

Wire for fastening to charge

kilogram charges.

40. The throwing radius for a concentrated charge is 10 to 15 yards. When throwing it, the soldier must consider the length of the fuze (about 1/2 inch burns in 1 second). The thrower aims at the tracks or at the belly of an approaching tank.

41. The concentrated charge can also be used as a multiple charge or as a slide-mine as described in paragraph 37 above.

42. If the charge is supposed to be used on top of the tank it must be secured so it will not fall off. For this purpose, its bottom is painted with warmed tar. If the charge is primed, be careful! A charge thus prepared will adhere to horizontal and even to slightly inclined surfaces. Putty can be used also for this purpose, but it is not reliable on wet surfaces.

Charges may be held on a tank by using an anchor made of strong wire, which is hooked into openings or protuberances of the vehicle (see figure 10).

43. The ignition for paragraphs 39 to 41 is provided by preparing short fuzes with detonating caps (to burn in 4 1/2 to 15 seconds), time fuzes, prima-cord, and wire for improvised pull igniter, or a pressure-igniter. The latter fastening is best suited for the destruction of tracks.

If the charge is thrown, a short fuze is needed (but at least 4 1/2 centimeters long, like a hand-grenade fuze). If it is placed on the tank, a 15-cm fuze is used for the security of the man placing it. *[1 centimeter of fuze burns in about 4 seconds.]*

Sliding Mines

44. Charges of 3 or 6 kilograms can be made and built into a two-sided skid. This sliding mine has to be secured against premature

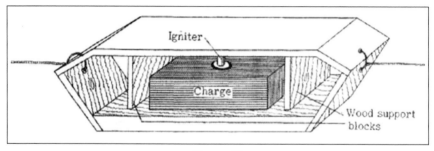

Figure 11

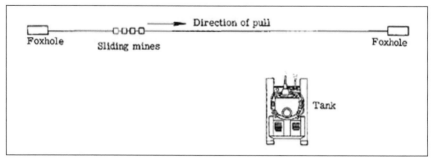

Figure 12

detonation, resulting from falling or turning over, by the insertion of two woodblocks (figure 11).

Two to four sliding mines are linked together and at each end of a given group is a 20-meter cable or rope.

Tank hunters sit in two foxholes about 20 meters apart. The sliding mines are camouflaged and placed somewhere between the holes so that they can be pulled in either direction. At the approach of a tank, they are pulled under its tracks (figure 12).

Several pairs of soldiers in similar foxholes can protect a larger area, for instance a key-point of resistance (figure 13).

Tellermines

45. Instead of concentrated charges, Tellermines [antitank mines] can be used, either as multiple charges or as sliding mines. However, as they have a high radius of fragmentation, they can only be worked from splinter-proof positions.

IV. Close-in Combat with Firearms

46. There should always be close cooperation between the tank-hunting squads and the other combat elements in the area. Discussion

144

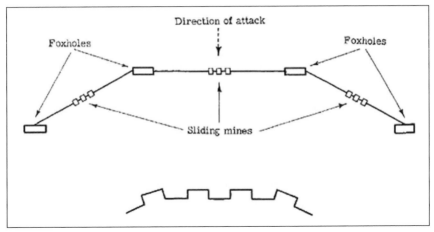

Figure 13

between the leader of the tank-destroyer squad and the leader of the other available arms is advisable in order to fix the beginning and end of the fire attack against a tank.

47. New [Russian?] tanks have especially strong armor at some points. But they have many weak spots, against which even the fire of weapons which are not armor-piercing can be successful. **It is therefore imperative to hit the tank not only as a whole, but especially at those weak spots.**

48. For this purpose, it is necessary that the rifleman, conscious of the power of his weapon and of his superiority over the tank, should keep cool. He must be able to open fire on the tank as late as possible, surprising it at the shortest possible distance. Courageous riflemen with rifle or antitank rifle, making full and skillful use of terrain, should crawl up to the best range.

The shorter the range, the greater the accuracy of the weapon. Also, the armor-piercing capacity of the ammunition will be increased.

When using armor-piercing ammunition, in order to ensure its successful use, it is important to follow closely the instructions found in the ammunition boxes concerning the aiming points and the effective range.

Opening fire as late as possible has the further advantage of keeping the weapon concealed from covering tanks and observers up to the decisive moment.

49. Frequently it will be advisable to concentrate the fire of several similar or different weapons on one tank e.g., rifles, a light machine gun, a heavy machine gun, an antitank gun, and a light infantry cannon. Ambush-like concentration of all weapons to surprise the tank is preferable. The physical and moral effect will be heightened by such concentration. If only a few tanks appear, it is preferable to assault them successively according to the danger presented by individual tanks. In the case of a massed attack, rigid fire control must insure that the most dangerous tanks are attacked simultaneously.

50. When several different weapons are combined against it, the tank will be blinded by the use of heavy machine-gun fire and small explosive grenades. At the same time, guns of 75-mm caliber and larger will fire against the tracks to cripple the tank. It is necessary to wait for a favorable moment, when for instance difficult terrain slows up the tank, or when it halts to fire. Once it is stopped, it will be destroyed by combined fire or by close-in assault.

51. Weapons with armor-piercing ammunition of smaller calibers are sometimes ineffective against tanks with sloping armor plates, even if their power of penetration would be great enough to pierce the plate if vertical. Because of the slope of the plates, the ammunition ricochets from the tank. On such tanks it is necessary to aim at the vertical parts.

Even in the case of vertical armor plates there will be an oblique angle of impact if a tank approaches at a sharp angle. In that case the angle of impact is also such that the projectiles will ricochet. Therefore, the tank should be fired upon at right angles. If the tank appears at an unfavorable angle, firing will be withheld until it assumes a more vulnerable position, either by revolving the turret or by actually turning and maneuvering.

52. It is possible to increase the effect and accuracy of fire by the selection of a flanking position, because the tanks are usually less strongly armed on the sides, and also offer a bigger target. Furthermore, vertical armor is more common on the sides than on the front.

53. Weak parts of tanks, against which fire from all arms is effective, are: vision slits, openings for hand weapons, periscopes, hatches, shutters, turret rings, ventilator openings, track, belly (the part of the hull between the tracks), and the engine cover (usually in the rear). The accurate location of these parts in the individual types can be found in the manuals.

54. Severe physical and moral effect can be achieved with the rifle, the light machine gun, and the heavy machine gun by firing heavy ball ammunition and armor-piercing ammunition at less than 300 yards against the weak parts of the tank, or by firing with submachine guns and armor-piercing grenades from a grenade discharger at very close range.

Projectiles hitting the vision slits or periscopes blind the crew, and prevent them from aiming or driving accurately. Also, small particles of molten lead and lead fumes penetrate into the interior of the tank and may injure the crew. Some bullets might jam the turret ring or weapon shutters so that revolving of the turret or firing the weapons will be made impossible.

As tanks are more poorly armored on top, attack from high points such as trees or houses will get better results.

The demoralizing effect on the crew of the noise of bullets hitting the tank surface should not be underestimated.

55. HE and armor-piercing grenades (impact fuzes) fired with the rifle grenade-launcher (flat trajectory), antitank guns up to a caliber of 50-mm, the 75-mm infantry howitzer, and the 150-mm infantry howitzer directed against the weak parts of a tank will have about the same results as described in the preceding paragraph. Furthermore the power of impact will cause the inside surface of the armor plates to splinter off and wound the crew. If the projectiles have high explosive charges like the heavy infantry howitzer, the crew will become casualties from the concussion, or they will be at least temporarily knocked out.

When firing against the engine cover in the rear with explosive shells of all weapons, an incendiary effect may be obtained under favorable circumstances. Light and heavy infantry howitzers attack the tracks most effectively.

The ranges for individual weapons have to be selected so that great accuracy of aim can be achieved. For small dispersion and flat trajectory the light and heavy infantry howitzers should use the maximum charge.

The turret, the side, and the rear of the tank are considered weak parts for armor-piercing ammunition. Armor-piercing weapons, unable to use armor-piercing ammunition, can effectively assist in the assault against tanks with high-explosive ammunition.

57. Destructive results in combat against armor are obtained with the 37-mm stick grenade or bomb. Its short range, however, results in success only at close distances.

V. Training

58. Training in close-in attack on tanks includes the knowledge of the weak parts, of the construction, use, and effect of close-in weapons, and of combat principles. To this purpose, instruction (using sand-table models and captured enemy tanks) and practical exercises are necessary. After the individual fighter has been trained, the cooperation of the squad and group in terrain exercises will be practiced. Combat exercises with live ammunition against large dummies or captured tanks will complete the training.

59. To improve accuracy in antitank fire, riflemen and gunners of all the arms (machine gun, antitank, infantry howitzer, field artillery) must know all vulnerable parts against which their weapons can be used effectively, and they must perform daily aiming exercises against tank models. Special practice is needed for the use of the Very pistol and rifle grenade. By the use of sub-caliber fire with antitank guns and practice firing with rifles and machine guns against tank models, and by combat exercises, marksmanship is to be developed to the utmost.

60. Each rifleman, whether he is part of a tank-hunting squad or the gunner of an individual weapon, must be thoroughly convinced that, if he fights skillfully he and his weapon are superior to any tank. He has to know that he is the hunter and the tank the game. This thought is to be given great weight in the training period.

VI. Assault Badge

The destruction of tanks in close-in combat counts as an assault. Rifemen, tank hunters, and other personnel who have fulfilled the necessary requirements in destroying tanks, will be awarded the assault badge.

23. GERMAN DEFENSIVE TACTICS IN RUSSIA

Tactical and Technical Trends,
No. 18, February 11th 1943

The following report contains German conclusions on certain phases of their defensive tactics as used in Russia.

a. Tanks should be kept in reserve. They should attack the flanks of enemy armored units as soon as the direction of the enemy attack is clear.

b. Defiladed antitank positions are highly desirable. Antitank guns should not open fire until approaching enemy tanks are at point-blank range. However, fire should be brought to bear under all circumstances, even though there appears to be little chance of success. The enemy tank will be slowed down, and will usually swing away. Antitank guns must be highly mobile so that they can be massed at any point where the enemy tanks are attacking. An allotment of half-track vehicles to antitank units is highly desirable to aid in obtaining cross-country mobility.

c. Concentrated artillery fire has a good harassing effect on enemy tanks.

Russian tank attacks are usually accompanied by infantry. German infantry which was passed by the tanks had great success against Russian infantry following the tanks. Therefore, all available means should be used to combat "tank shock." Experience has shown that German infantry when Russian tanks passed through them suffered only slight casualties when they were in "dug-in" positions. For this reason it is essential that foxholes be dug deep, and at once, by every means available.

24. GERMAN TACTICS - RUSSIAN FRONT

Tactical and Technical Trends,
No. 18, February 11th 1943

The following report deals with the experiences of the German Army on the Eastern Front. The extracts are taken from two documents issued by The German War Office, one dated March 1, 1942, and the other August 1, 1942.

a. Attack

The special nature of the Russian Front, with its great area and few roads, has led to a tendency when on the march to cling too much to existing roads. The Russians have based their defensive system on these roads. The best attack is that made off the roads, using enveloping forces which must be made as strong as possible. Where possible, artillery should be allocated to these enveloping forces, but in most cases they will have to depend for their fire power on the heavy weapons of the infantry, especially the heavy mortars. Even weak enveloping forces may achieve decisive results by surprise attack, coordinated with the main frontal attack.

The fighting in the Kerch Peninsula has once more shown that deep slit trenches, and well-built earthworks, often render impossible the destruction of the enemy by artillery, infantry support weapons, and by bombing; these, as a rule, serve only to make the enemy keep his head down. Infantry in the attack must, therefore, approach as closely as possible behind the artillery barrage, and attack with all possible speed as soon as it is lifted.

The Russians have shown themselves very susceptible to a section or platoon assault in close formation, carried out with shouts and firing on the move.

Night attacks have been found to be of special importance on the Eastern Front, since it is the Russian practice to carry out moves at night, and these attacks prevent the enemy from carrying out his plan.

b. Coordination of the Various Arms

On the Russian Front our success in the coordination of the various arms has been due to the careful organization of the fire plan of all weapons down to those of even the smallest units. The infantry must learn not to rely exclusively on artillery fire, or the support of tanks or assault guns, but must use its own heavy weapons to the fullest extent.

The main task of the artillery is counterbattery missions, and all available forces will be concentrated against the enemy's artillery "schwerpunkt" (area in which enemy artillery is concentrated) without regard to corps or divisional boundaries.

Assault guns must never be used without the protection given by accompanying troops. They require infantry protection since, as they have no revolving turret and little protective armor, they are incapable of close defense.

c. Defense

Russian reconnaissance is pushed without regard to losses. Limited attacks for purposes of reconnaissance, are, as a rule, carried out mostly by a company, but may be made by a battalion. When the weak spots are thus found, the enemy maneuvers his main forces, which are usually masses of infantry supported by tanks. The attack is preceded by intensified mortar fire, and shelling by tanks at extreme ranges. If the leading tanks are shot up and the first attack beaten off, a pause of several hours often precedes the second attack.

The rule for defense in open country, when ammunition is plentiful, is to open fire at great ranges; when the country is not open and ammunition is scarce, it is more effective to let the enemy approach, and then strike him with sudden concentrated fire at long range.

Defense on a wide front is the rule on the Eastern Front, where only the most important points can be occupied. These are to be built up as strongpoints, and occupied with one or more platoons, with heavy weapons (heavy mortars, heavy machine guns, and antitank guns). All-around defense must be organized. When the strongpoints are far apart, greater patrol activities between them will be necessary.

d. Antitank Defense

Russian tanks seldom attack in large numbers. As a rule a few, sometimes even single, tanks precede the attacking infantry, which then follows in compact groups. In defense, therefore, the most important task of all arms is to separate the infantry from the tanks. The aim of infantry training in antitank defense must be to teach the young soldier that the effect of tanks against dug-in riflemen is extraordinarily limited. Fighting against tanks is, for the infantrymen, merely a matter of nerves.

The plan for antitank defense should ensure that 50-mm antitank guns are brought into position in good time, because of their lack of mobility; 37-mm antitank guns may be held on carts under cover, or near prepared positions, since these guns are more mobile.

e. March Discipline

The few and very bad roads in the east have necessarily had heavy traffic, and a column moving on the roads is liable to become very extended. Therefore, troops following up require more time than usual, and it is necessary to put well to the front of the column considerable detachments of artillery and heavy weapons, and communications and engineer personnel. Similarly, to ensure the supply of a column, carefully calculated loads of ammunition, fuel, and lubricants must be included at intervals along the road.

f. Night Fighting

In night attacks all units must be given definite and limited objectives. Detailed and careful planning is the basis of success, and considerable previous reconnaissance is required. The result; of this reconnaissance form the basis of the commander's plan, which must be known down to its smallest details by every junior commander.
A useful means of keeping direction at night is the preliminary setting of fire to haystacks or houses in enemy territory.

g. Mobile Troops

Fighting over wide, open areas and along roads has often made necessary the formation of mixed battle groups in which tanks have been included. As a consequence, the number of tanks decreased rapidly and the units from which they were detached lacked the necessary strength to carry out independent attacks. An armored division equipped with a tank regiment of three battalions and motorized infantry is capable of extensive tasks, provided its tanks are kept concentrated, and the motorized infantry is directed to cooperate closely.

In defense the most successful method of stopping a breakthrough of enemy mobile troops or tanks is the formation of mobile groups reinforced with antitank and close-support weapons; they should be disposed in depth throughout the sector, particularly in localities vulnerable to tanks. These counterattack groups are to be held ready to attack the flank or rear of any enemy force which may break through and to cut off the enemy rearward communications.

h. Miscellaneous

For all infantry weapons, in particular the machine gun, mortar, and antitank gun, a wide field of fire is not so important as emplacement to produce a heavy uninterrupted belt of fire to the immediate front.

On the Eastern Front, unnecessary losses have been caused by unmilitary behavior, both at headquarters and in units, in zones covered by enemy fire. Considerable casualties, which could have been avoided, have been caused by the disinclination of the German soldier to dig in quickly in the course of the battle, his carelessness behind the immediate front, and by inadequate battle reconnaissance of invisible areas.

25. EMPLOYMENT OF GERMAN ANTIAIRCRAFT ARTILLERY AT SEVASTOPOL

Tactical and Technical Trends, No. 7, September 10th 1942

The account given below describes an interesting example of the employment of antiaircraft guns in the battle for Sevastopol. This article appeared in the German press in the middle of June, and shows clearly that 88-mm antiaircraft guns have been used against ground targets by the German troops in Russia just as they have been by the Afrika Korps of Field Marshal Rommel.

"The battle for Sevastopol is among the hardest of the war. Here the German Command was confronted with a narrow front barricaded completely with concrete, steel, and guns. But however heavy the barrage from the massed Soviet artillery, our antiaircraft guns succeeded in pushing through on several occasions and knocking out pillboxes at very short ranges so that our infantry could advance again. The initiative of the antiaircraft gun crews in the battle for Sevastopol was outstanding, and one particular instance has been singled out as an example.

"A lieutenant in charge of an antiaircraft combat detachment, who had been especially prominent in the fighting on the northern sector of the Sevastopol front, was ordered to support the infantry attack with one heavy gun and a light antiaircraft section, firing from a gully. The tasks of these antiaircraft combat detachments are almost always extraordinarily difficult. While the field artillery remains stationary for long periods in each position, the guns of the antiaircraft combat groups move close behind the first wave of the infantry, and engage over open sights and at very short ranges those pillboxes and other enemy centers of resistance which the infantry cannot overcome. Since the antiaircraft groups move normally without cover, they tend to draw the fire of all the enemy artillery. Such was the case here—

and, in addition, the Soviet defenders had registered every yard of the ground.

"At first the task seemed impossible to the lieutenant. There was no field of fire for his gun from the gully, and the violent fire of the defenders made it impossible to advance. All alternative routes to the enemy pillboxes were also under heavy fire.

"Thereupon; the lieutenant decided on a bold gamble. Despite the intensive Soviet fire, he rushed his gun to a suitable position and opened fire immediately. By constant change of position and by taking cover momentarily when things became too hot, he was able to maintain an almost continuous rate of fire against his targets. In this way he succeeded in knocking out six pillboxes and, in conjunction with the light antiaircraft section, silenced a number of field works, machine-gun nests, and gun positions.

"Similar antiaircraft combat groups were employed on a number of other sectors. In practically every instance they are the first heavy weapons to follow the infantry. Although the way is first cleared for them by the engineers, it nevertheless requires skill and coolness to take the gun through the narrow gap in the minefields, where the slightest deviation may bring disaster. Furthermore the terrain at Sevastopol is extremely difficult. The long hillsides are covered with thick undergrowth and bushes, and bristle with pillboxes and weapon-pits. Concealed Russian snipers will permit the antiaircraft elements to pass unmolested and then ambush the supporting units as they come up. The German infantry, following its own artillery screen on a front of a few hundred yards, is subjected to continuous Soviet attacks, supported by artillery, from the flank. In these circumstances the situation has often been saved solely by the initiative of the antiaircraft combat groups and by the high rate of fire of their guns."

Comment:

The above account appears to indicate that the Germans, at any rate at Sevastopol, used antiaircraft guns to give close support to the infantry. The high velocity and heavy shell of the 88-mm antiaircraft gun make it a formidable weapon against pillboxes and similar types of concrete defenses.

26. RUSSIAN EMPLOYMENT OF ANTIAIRCRAFT GUNS AGAINST TANKS

Tactical and Technical Trends,
No. 7, September 10th 1942

Like the Germans, the Russians have found that it is profitable to allot antiaircraft guns a secondary mission of antitank defense. The following comments on antitank employment of these guns are taken from a recent issue of the semiofficial "Red Star".

"In the Russo-German War the Red Army antiaircraft artillery has learned to combat tanks as well as planes. Dual-purpose antiaircraft guns make good antitank guns because of their high muzzle velocity, high rate of fire, and 360° traverse.

"In the first 6 months of the war, Red Army antiaircraft artillery fired in self-defense at enemy tanks which broke through to the battery positions. Gradually, however, the antiaircraft artillery became an organic part of the antitank defensive system. In numerous instances, Russian antiaircraft guns have successfully repulsed attacks of large tank units.

"The antiaircraft units learned that most tactical operations seem to divide themselves into two phases. In the first phase, Russian army artillery concentrates heavy fire on enemy tanks before they can jump off. It then lays down a screen of fire to prevent the enemy tanks from approaching the Russian forward line of defense and breaking up infantry formations. In this stage the antiaircraft units are busily engaged in repelling the attacks of enemy aircraft, particularly dive bombers, which attempt to open the way for the tanks.

"In the second phase, after German tanks have broken into the initial line of defense, or deeper, the German aviation generally shifts its attention to Russian units reserved for counterattack. In this comparative lull, antiaircraft guns fire at the German tanks by direct laying; the shorter the range, the more effective the fire.

"It must always be remembered, however, that the first mission of antiaircraft artillery is defense against planes. In areas where there is insufficient antitank artillery, antiaircraft guns must be employed to drive off tanks which approach the battery positions or threaten to break up the battle formations of Russian troops.

"In order to combat enemy mechanized forces successfully, the antiaircraft artillery must prepare its antitank defense in advance. When the guns go into position they must be ready to open fire against attacking tanks immediately. To establish such a system it is necessary to:

1) Make a complete study of the surrounding terrain, with particular regard to possible tank approaches;
2) Determine the sector of fire for each gun, including ranges to key reference points;
3) Build the minimum amount of field fortifications necessary;
4) Establish special antitank observation points.

"All antiaircraft personnel not working at the guns during a tank attack take up positions in the vicinity and use hand grenades, gasoline bottles, or small-arms armor-piercing bullets against the enemy tanks."

27. GERMAN 75-MM ASSAULT GUN

Tactical and Technical Trends,
No. 7, September 10th 1942

This assault gun is a self-propelled gun mounted on a standard Mark III tank chassis. In 1940 a relatively small number took part in the Battle of France and it was first used extensively in the summer of 1941, when it played an important tactical role in the first battles on the Russian front.

The guns are organized into independent battalions, although it is now possible that they are organic within the motorized and Panzer divisions and are attached to front-line infantry divisions. Normally only direct fire is used.

An assault gun captured in the Middle East is described below.

The gun and mount weigh about 20 tons.

The gun itself is the short-barreled 75-mm tank gun originally mounted in the Mark IV tank. The range drum is graduated for HE up to 6,550 yards and for AP up to 1,640 yards. Elevation and traverse are hand-operated. Some other details are these:

Length of bore	23.5 cals.
Muzzle velocity (estimated)	1,600 f.s.
Elevation	20°
Depression	5°
Traverse	20°
Weight of projectiles	
HE	12 lb. 9 oz.
Smoke	13 lb. 9 oz
AP (with ballistic cap)	13 lb.9 oz.
AP (hollow charge)	not known
Estimated penetration of AP (with ballistic cap)	55 mm. (2.16 in.) at 60°at 400 yds.

7·5 cm STURMGESCHÜTZ

(75-MM ASSAULT GUN)

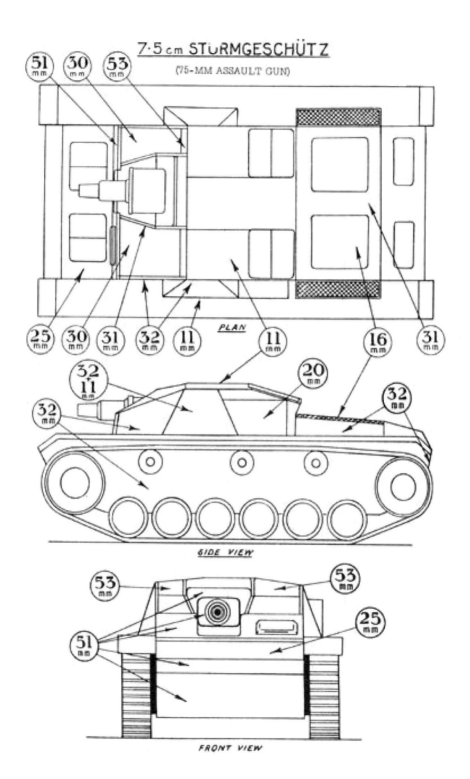

PLAN

SIDE VIEW

FRONT VIEW

160

It is believed that this low-velocity gun is being replaced by a high-velocity 75-mm gun with a reported length of bore of about 43 calibers. The Germans are also apparently making a similar change in the armament of the Mark IV Tank.

As stated above, the hull is that of the standard German Mark III tank with normal suspension system. The turret has been removed. The length is 17 ft. 9 in., height 6 ft. 5 in., and width 9 ft. 7 in. In general the armor is 51 mm. (2 in.) at the front and 32 mm. (1.25 in.) on the sides and at the rear. An added 53-mm plate is fitted to the rear of the front vertical plate, apparently between the driving and fighting compartments, and is braced to the front plate by two 31-mm. plates, one on each side of the opening for the gun. For detailed arrangement of armor plate see accompanying sketch.

The sides of the hull are reported to be vulnerable to the British 40-mm antitank gun at 1,500 yards, but this gun can penetrate the front only at very short ranges, and even then only the driving compartment.

The engine is a Maybach V-12-type rated at 300 horsepower. The gears provide for six speeds, and steering is hydraulically controlled. The capacity of the gasoline tank is 71 gallons, which is consumed at the rate of about 0.9 miles per gallon at a cruising speed of 22 miles per hour. The radius of action is about 70 miles, the maximum rate of speed about 29 miles per hour.

As in German tanks, this vehicle is equipped to carry extra gasoline in a rack on the rear of the vehicle, which should hold about 10 standard 5-gallon gasoline cans.

The captured vehicle contained metal boxes for 44 rounds of ammunition, and 40 rounds were stacked on the floor at the loader's station. Ammunition is also carried in an armored half-track which tows an armored ammunition trailer. There was also a rack for 12 stick grenades, and the usual smoke-candle release mechanism for 5 candles was fitted to the rear. For communication there were two radio receivers and one transmitter. For observation a scissors telescope was provided.

As spare parts the 11-mm. sloping plates over the track guard (see sketch) carried two spare bogie wheels on the right side and one on the left side. Two spare torsion rods were also carried, one in each side of the hull above the bogies.

The crew consists of four men — a commander, gunner, loader, and driver.

28. BREAKTHROUGH AGAINST GERMAN DEFENSES

Tactical and Technical Trends, No. 10, October 22nd 1942

The German defensive system employed on one sector of the Eastern Front and the methods employed by Soviet infantry and artillery units in breaking through these defenses are described in the following article written by a Red Army officer:

"In many battles on the Leningrad front, it has been ascertained that the German system of defense is usually based on the establishment of a series of separate firing points which mutually support each other. In one small operation, the distinguishing characteristics of their defenses were irregularity of pattern, and the width of front covered in establishing these firing points. They were placed along two general lines. Some had embrasures and overhead cover while others were open. At distances from 50 to 200 yards in the rear were dugouts used for rest purposes, or for protection from artillery and machine-gun fire.

"In the forward firing points were the German light and heavy machine guns. Some of these were protected by a single row of barbed wire. In the rear firing points were mortars and light artillery. All firing points were assigned regular and supplementary sectors of fire. The sectors were overlapping and, in the case of machine guns, final protective lines were interlocking. Initial fire adjustment was made on the east bank of the river, the Soviet jump-off line. Mortar fire was used en masse and was shifted from target to target. In their retreat the Germans had burned all villages on the east bank of the river, thus materially improving their observation and field of fire.

"After careful study of the terrain and the enemy defenses, the Red Army regimental commander decided to strike at the enemy center of resistance near the church. After it had been reduced, it would then be possible to make a flank attack to the north, or to strike at the village held by the 6th Company of the German infantry. The local defenses of the latter comprised only four completed firing points, which were occupied by two light and two heavy machine guns. Two of the emplacements were of the open type, and communication between them and to the rear was difficult because of the heavy brush.

"On the morning of the attack, the Red Army infantry was deployed along the east bank of the river. After the artillery preparation, during which the Germans followed their customary practice of taking cover in their dugouts on the rear slopes, the infantry jumped off at dawn. As the artillery fire was lifted to the rear firing points and enemy reserve concentrations, our mortars and machine guns placed direct fire on the forward firing points. The result was that the Germans were so pinned down that they were unable to get back to their firing positions. Our small-arms weapons which were brought forward proceeded to destroy the effectiveness of the forward firing points by direct fire at the embrasures. Meanwhile, the artillery and mortars kept up neutralizing fire on the rear firing points.

"Attacking in formation of two battalions in line, one in reserve, our leading company was able to capture the enemy positions near the church. It was then possible for the remainder of the two attacking battalions, with supporting artillery and machine-gun fire, to develop their attack to the north and to southwest. By committing his reserve battalion at the proper time, the Red Army commander succeeded in occupying all three villages by noon.

"Several important conclusions may be drawn from the above tactical operation. First of all, it is necessary to utilize every means of reconnaissance to discover as nearly as possible the exact positions of the enemy's forward firing points and his main line of resistance. A plan for coordinated infantry-artillery action must then be drawn up. In this plan it is essential to designate which unit will dispose of each individual firing point, and when and how it will be done. Reserve units must be designated to deal with new firing points as they are discovered.

"Fire and movement are still the cardinal principles of infantry, down to the last rifleman. They must eliminate enemy riflemen, machine-gun nests, etc. as they move forward across the battlefield. They must use every means to discover and destroy the enemy before he can employ direct fire.

"The artillery is not the only arm which can neutralize a firing point. Infantry with light mortar, machine-gun, and automatic rifle fire can also be used to this end, especially in cases where the enemy's cover is light or non-existent. It is necessary to have good observation of the field of fire for our infantry and to deny the same to the enemy. If these precepts are followed, fire superiority and the success of the attack will be assured."

29. RUSSIAN ANTITANK TACTICS

Tactical and Technical Trends, No. 19, February 25th 1942

No particular reference to any specific engagement was made in the report which follows, though the subject dealt with is based on information received from the Russian front and published in the Red Army newspaper "Red Star."

Antitank tactics as practiced by the Russians are based on the essential need to separate the tanks from their supporting infantry. The German tactics of exploitation very often give opportunities of achieving this object. During the earlier phases of the war, before the Russians had realized the best methods of dealing with the enemy armored formations, the deep thrusts of the German "Panzers" actually did cause a certain amount of disintegration, but by the time the outer defenses of Moscow were reached these thrusts failed to achieve their object.

Russian infantry are trained to stop tanks if possible, but when it appears that the infantry are going to be overrun, they get into slit trenches and lie low until the waves of tanks have gone through. Then they come out and put up the strongest possible resistance against the German infantry to prevent it from maintaining contact with the tanks. The artillery is trained to operate on exactly the same lines; if the gun position is overrun, crews go to earth and re-man their guns as soon as the tanks have passed them.

Once the tanks, in rear of the Russian positions, have been cut off from their supporting infantry, every effort is made to prevent their retirement and to mop them up. Mobile antitank groups are formed to harry them, and whenever they go into bivouac, the nearest infantry are instructed to attack them, particularly at night. In fact, whenever tanks are known to be halted in the vicinity, infantry tank-hunting parties are sent to engage them. The air force is always called upon to cooperate extensively in this mopping-up phase.

30. GERMAN TANK MAINTENANCE AND RECOVERY

Tactical and Technical Trends, No. 10, October 22nd 1942

Some of the maintenance units attached to German tank regiments were discussed briefly in Tactical and Technical Trends No. 4, p. 10. More information is now available on these units and is presented here in a summary which involves some revision of the earlier material.

a. Organization

In the German armored divisions, the maintenance and recovery units are ordinarily organized as follows:

(1) Company Repair Section

Each tank company has a repair section consisting of:

- 1 NCO (tank mechanic), section leader,
- 3 NCO's, tank mechanics,
- 13 privates, tank mechanics,
- 2 privates, tank radio electricians,
- 1 private, armorer's assistant,
- 4 privates, chauffeurs.
  Total: 4 NCO's and 20 EM.

This repair section has the following vehicles:

- 1 small repair car (Kfz. 2/40),
- 1 medium cross-country repair truck, for spare parts and tools,
- 2 half-track vehicles (Sd. Kfz. 10) for personnel, capable of towing 1 ton,
- 3 motorcycles with sidecars.

(2) Battalion and Regimental Repair Sections

The headquarters of each tank battalion and each tank regiment has a repair section consisting of:

- 1 NCO (tank mechanic), section leader,
- 3 privates, tank mechanics (for a tank regimental headquarters),

or
- 5 privates, tank mechanics 7for a tank battalion headquarters),
- 1 private, motorcyclist, tank radio electrician,
- 1 private, chauffeur, tank radio electrician,
- 1 chauffeur.

   Total: for Hq, tank regiment, 1 NCO and 6 men;
              for Hq, tank battalion, 1 NCO and 8 men.

This repair section has the following vehicles:
- 1 small repair car (Kfz. 2/40),
- 1 medium cross-country repair truck, for spare parts and tools,
- 1 motorcycle with sidecar.

(3) Workshop Company

A captured German document gives the following detailed organization of a Panzer workshop company, as of September 15, 1941. It is believed that the organization given in this document is not that of tank units in a particular theater but has general application.

The document sets forth the organization of a workshop company in a Panzer regiment with six companies (as in Libya), but makes provision for added strength (as noted below) in regiments of eight companies, and in regiments of three battalions.

(a) Headquarters Platoon
- 1 cross-country truck (Kfz. 1) — 1 chauffeur, 1 company commander (engineer), 1 officer for special duties (engineer), 1 clerk (draftsman). (One of the two officers may be other than an engineer officer.)
- 1 motorcycle — 1 motorcyclist (orderly).
- 1 medium truck — 1 chauffeur, 2 men for salvaging spare parts (M) [Here, and later, where the meaning of technical abbreviations is not certain, they are given as they appear in the document.]
- 1 light personnel car — 1 chauffeur, 1 official (K-motor transport), 1 NCO for spare parts, 1 clerk (asst. chauffeur).
- 1 motorcycle with sidecar — 1 motorcyclist (orderly), 1 foreman for motor transport equipment (Maybach Specialist).

(b) 1st and 2d Platoons

- 1 motor bus (Kraftomnibus)
- 1 chauffeur, 4 NCO's for workshop service (Vorh.W.=craftsmen?)
- 1 tank electrician and mechanic, 1 tank electric welder, 1 saddler, 1 tinsmith, 1 carpenter, 1 painter, 7 tank motor mechanics, 3 tank transmission mechanics, 1 automobile mechanic, 1 clerk.
- 5 medium trucks, for spare parts and assemblies
- (each) 1 chauffeur, 1 tank transmission mechanic (asst. chauffeur), 1 automobile mechanic.
- 1 medium truck for spare parts and assemblies
- 1 chauffeur, 1 NCO in charge of spare parts, 1 depot chief (M).
- 1 truck with special workshop and trailer for arc-welding apparatus
- 1 chauffeur, 1 NCO for workshop service (vorhandwk), 1 tank electric welder (asst. chauffeur).
- 1 heavy truck, tools and equipment
- 1 chauffeur, 1 tank motor mechanic, 1 blacksmith.
- 1 workshop truck (Kfz.19), with trailer for heavy machine apparatus, Set A
- 1 chauffeur, 1 foreman (leader), 1 turner.

(c) 3d Platoon (Recovery Platoon)

- 1 light cross-country automobile (Kfz. 1)
- 1 chauffeur, 1 officer (platoon leader), NCO (Panzer-Wart, tank mechanic)
- 1 medium cross-country truck (Kfz. 100) for towing apparatus, with rotating crane (3 tons) [A note on the document states that this apparatus will be delivered later.]
- 1 chauffeur, 1 asst. chauffeur (automobile mechanic).
- 1 medium half-track prime mover (8 tons)
- 1 chauffeur, 1 assistant chauffeur (automobile mechanic).
- 2 medium half-track prime movers (8 tons) with underslung trailers (10 tons)
- (each) 1 chauffeur, 1 asst. chauffeur (mechanic), and (for one

only of these trucks) 1 NCO (tank mechanic).

- 2 vehicles (with apparatus) [The designation of this apparatus and the vehicle model number are not clear on the original document. The apparatus is designated as not yet available. The vehicles are apparently heavy half-track prime movers.] (6 tons, Sd. Kfz. 41)
- (each) 1 chauffeur, 1 assistant chauffeur (automobile mechanic).
- 5 heavy half-track prime movers (18 tons), with underslung trailers (20 tons)
- (each) 1 chauffeur, 1 assistant chauffeur (automobile mechanic), 1 steerer for trailer; one prime mover has in addition, an NCO (tank mechanic).
- 2 motorcycles with sidecars
- (each) 1 chauffeur (tank mechanic), 1 NCO (tank mechanic).
- (One of the NCO's is second in command.)
  (d) Armory Section
- 1 medium cross-country automobile (Kfz. 15 m.G.)
- 1 chauffeur, 2 armorers (one is section leader), 1 armorer's helper.
- 1 motorcycle with sidecar
- 1 NCO armorer (0), 1 helper.
- 3 vehicles (not described), for armorer's tools
- One with 1 chauffeur, 1 NCO, armorer (0), 1 tank electrician and mechanic (asst. chauffeur);
- One with 1 chauffeur, 1 tank electrician (asst. chauffeur), 1 armorer's helper;
- One with 1 chauffeur, 2 armorer's helpers (one is asst. chauffeur).
- 1 light cross-country car for supply of tools
- 1 chauffeur, 1 armorer's helper.
  (e) Workshops for Communications Equipment
- 1 battery-charging truck (Kfz. 42) *[According to the document, there is a trailer attached to this truck, but no description is given.]*
- 1 chauffeur, 1 NCO mechanic (leader), 1 mechanic.

- 1 communications workshop truck (Kfz. 42) [An ambiguous note suggests that this equipment had not yet been delivered.]
- 1 chauffeur, 1 mechanic (asst. chauffeur).
- 1 light cross-country truck
- 1 chauffeur, 1 mechanic (asst. chauffeur).

  (f) Company Supply
- 1 medium truck for rations and baggage
- 1 chauffeur, 1 NCO in charge of equipment (leader).
- 1 motorcycle with sidecar
- 1 supply sergeant (K), 1 clerk (asst. motorcyclist).
- 1 antiaircraft truck (Kfz. 4)
- 1 chauffeur, 1 NCO (in charge), 1 machine-gunner.
- 2 medium trucks for fuel
- One, with 1 chauffeur and 1 tailor (asst. chauffeur);
- One, with 1 chauffeur and 1 shoemaker (asst. chauffeur).
- 2 medium trucks for large field-kitchen stoves
- One, with 1 chauffeur, 1 NCO in charge of rations (asst. chauffeur), 1 cook, 1 asst. cook;
- One, with 1 chauffeur, 1 NCO (accountant), 1 NCO (cook), 1 asst. cook (asst. chauffeur).
- 1 light automobile
- 1 chauffeur (clerk), 1 master sergeant, 1 medical officer.

  Total Strength of Workshop Company

3 officers, 5 officials, [Only one official is designated as such in the preceding breakdown of the company's organization. If the foreman and depot chief in each of the 1st and 2d Platoons are officials, this would clear up the discrepancy.] 29 NCO's, 158 EM (total, 195 men) and 1 shop foreman for motor transport equipment (group leader).

(h) The document makes the following provisions for enlargement of the workshop company:

(1) For tank regiments with three battalions, add one workshop platoon (same organization as 1st Platoon above). Add to the Recovery Platoon two heavy half-track prime movers (18 tons) with 22-ton trailers, each to have 1 chauffeur, 1 asst. chauffeur (automobile mechanic), 1 trailer steerer. This involves additional

personnel of 1 official, 6 NCO's, 49 EM - total, 56 men. The workshop company then has a total strength of 251 men.

(2) For tank regiments with 4 companies in a battalion (i.e., two battalions to the regiment), add:

To each of the 1st and 2d Platoons — 2 medium trucks for spare parts, each with 1 chauffeur and 1 motor mechanic (asst. chauffeur).

To the Recovery Platoon — 1 half-track prime mover (18 tons) with trailer (22 tons), and personnel of 1 chauffeur, 1 asst. chauffeur (automobile mechanic), and 1 trailer steerer.

(4) Light Workshop Platoon

According to pre-war organization, a tank regiment of three battalions had (in addition to the workshop company) a regimental workshop platoon. This unit comprised 1 officer, 2 officials, 3 NCO's, and 48 EM; the vehicles consisted of 1 automobile, 13 trucks (5 to 7 with trailers), and 3 motorcycles with sidecars.

There has been little available information on the workshop platoon since 1940. It is believed that the unit has been enlarged.

A captured document from Africa (1941) gives detailed instructions for a workshop platoon in a two-battalion tank regiment of the Africa Korps (which normally would not have this unit). In this case, an example of the flexibility of German organization, the personnel assigned to the platoon was obtained by breaking up the battalion headquarters repair sections of the two battalions. This workshop platoon was smaller than normal and was to operate, in place of the battalion headquarters repair sections, under command of the regiment.

The platoon was composed of:
- 1 sergeant mechanic (platoon leader),
- 1 Maybach specialist (for engines and Variorex gears),
- 2 NCO's tank mechanics (one an engine mechanic and electrician, the other to be also a welder),
- 2 tank mechanics,
- 1 car chauffeur,
- 2 motorcyclists (mechanics),

- 3 truck chauffeurs.
- The platoon had the following equipment in vehicles:
- 1 light cross-country automobile (for platoon leader and Maybach Specialist),
- 2 motorcycles with side cars (for the two NCO's),
- 1 truck with repair equipment (for 1 mechanic, 1 tank fitter),
- 2 trucks with materials and spare parts (each for 1 mechanic, 1 tank fitter),
- 1 light two-wheeled trailer,
- 1 trailer with reserve of oxygen and acetylene containers.

(5) According to pre-war organization, each armored division had, as part of divisional services, 3 divisional workshop companies. These companies would, on occasion, presumably aid the workshop units of the tank regiments, but information on this function is not available.

b. Functions of Tank Repair and Workshop Units

(1) The repair sections (the available information apparently applies to both types of repair section mentioned above) are responsible for the general maintenance of the tanks, and of their armament and radio apparatus.

In camp and rest areas, they keep a check upon the serviceability of vehicles in the unit to which they are attached; during this period, mechanics are given advanced training through attachment to the workshop company or under master-mechanics transferred to the unit.

On the march, repair sections travel with the tank units and deal with any breakdowns in vehicles or equipment, in so far as these repairs can be effected in less than 4 hours and with field equipment. If a tank breaks down, the repair section leader inspects it and determines the nature of the damage. If the damage warrants it, the tank is handed over to the recovery platoon to be towed away; otherwise, a motorcycle with mechanics stays with the tank to effect repairs, while the other elements of the repair section go on with the column. In this way, one vehicle after another of the repair section stays behind; ordinarily the motorcycles, but, if damage is serious, a half-tracked vehicle. The repair automobile always goes on with the column, while the repair truck always stays with the repair vehicle left farthest to the rear.

In the assembly area, the repair sections thoroughly test all tanks and equipment as to fitness for battle. Any breakdowns are reported at once to the unit motor-transport sergeant.

In battle, the company repair sections are under the order of the battalion commander and are directed by a battalion motor-transport officer. As a rule they follow closely behind the fighting units and range over the battle area looking for broken-down tanks. If the tank cannot be repaired on the spot it is made towable and its position reported to the recovery platoon (of the workshop company).

In one tank battalion in Libya, an armor-repair section was added to the normal repair sections. The personnel was made up of armorer mechanics detached from other repair units, and included an armorer sergeant, an armorer corporal, and seven armorer's assistants. The equipment included an automobile, a motorcycle, and two trucks. This section was to follow the tanks in battle and to work with repair sections on weapons and turrets.

Repair sections are not allowed to undertake the welding of armor gashes longer than 4 inches. In battle, the regimental headquarters repair section is attached to a battalion.

(2) The armored workshop company operates as far as 15 to 20 miles behind the fighting tanks of its regiment, except that the recovery platoon works in the battle area, mainly to tow out disabled tanks.

The workshop company handles heavier repair jobs, up to those requiring 12 hours. Repair jobs requiring up to 24 hours are sent back to rear repair bases.

The workshop company has its own power tools, a crane, and apparatus for electric welding and vulcanizing. Its platoons may be separated, and may operate independently. According to one captured document, a workshop company dealt with 18 tanks in 17 days, under conditions where there was no shortage of spare parts.

(3) The light workshop platoon in the Afrika Korps tank regiment (discussed earlier) replaced the battalion headquarters repair sections and operated under command of the regiment as a connecting link between the workshop company and the company repair sections. Like the latter, it would handle work requiring less than 4 hours. In attack, this platoon would follow along the central axis of advance, in close touch with the recovery platoon of the workshop company.

The platoon was to carry out work as follows: on brakes, gears, and clutches of Mark II (light) tanks; on damaged gear-mechanism of Mark III tanks; and on valve defects of all types of truck and tank engines except Mark III and IV tanks. They were to remove electrical and fuel-system faults; salvage and tow wheeled vehicles; make repairs on wheeled vehicles; perform autogene welding and soldering work; and charge and test batteries and electrical apparatus.

c. Tank Recovery Methods

All observers stress the efficiency of the German recovery and maintenance units. The following points have been noted:

(1) The Germans will use combat tanks to tow disabled tanks in case of retirement; even during a battle, instances are reported, both from France and Africa, where combat tanks were employed both to protect towing operations and to assist in the towing. The recovery platoon, with its trailers, is not given the whole burden of this main job of salvage.

(2) The same principle of cooperation prevails on repair jobs in the field. Tanks carry many tools, spare parts, and equipment for repair work, and observers believe that the tank crews are trained to assist the repair crews as well as to service and maintain their own vehicles.

Not only is the recovery of German vehicles very efficient, but units will often send out detachments to recover those of the enemy. For instance, a tank battalion may send out a detachment consisting of an officer, one or two NCO's, and six or eight men, transported in one or two cross-country vehicles and protected by one or two light tanks, to search for and recover disabled hostile vehicles.

31. TACTICAL EMPLOYMENT OF GERMAN 75-MM ASSAULT GUN

Tactical and Technical Trends, No. 19, February 25th 1942

The German 75-mm assault gun (7.5-cm Sturmgeschütz) is a weapon comparable to the U.S. 75-mm and 105-mm self-propelled guns. The gun and mount weigh about 20 tons. Its maximum speed cross-country is about 7 mph, on roads about 22 mph; it can average about 15 mph. On normal roads its radius of action is about 100 miles, cross-country about 50 miles. To move an assault-gun battery 100 kilometers (about 65 miles) requires 4,000 liters (about 1,050 gallons) of gasoline. The range of the 75-mm short-barrelled tank gun (7.5-cm KwK), with which this weapon was originally equipped, is about 6,000 yards.

It is reported that there are now apparently three types of assault guns in service. These are: the Stu.G. 7.5-cm K, mounting the 7.5-cm KwK (short-barreled tank gun — 23.5 calibers [Length of bore]); the Stu.G. lg. 7.5-cm K, mounting the 7.5-cm KwK 40 (long-barreled tank gun — 43 calibers); and a third weapon, nomenclature at present unknown, which appears to have a 75-mm gun with a bore 30 calibers in length. It seems probable, therefore, that the 7.5-cm KwK 40, which is the principal armament of the new Pz. Kw. 4 (Mark IV tank), may be primarily an antitank weapon, while the latest intermediate gun will take the place of the old Stu.G. 7.5-cm K as a close-support weapon.

While some technical details of this weapon have been known for some time, relatively little information has been available until recently concerning its tactical employment. Two German documents on the tactical use of this weapon have now been received. One is dated May 1940, the other April 1942. The second document is essentially identical in substance with the first, except that the second contains some additional information. Both documents have been combined into one for the present report, and such apparent contradictions as exist are noted in the translation which follows.

INSTRUCTIONS FOR THE EMPLOYMENT OF ASSAULT ARTILLERY

a. BASIC PRINCIPLES AND ROLE

The assault gun (7.5-cm gun on an armored self-propelled mount) is an offensive weapon. It can fire only in the general direction in which the vehicle is pointing *[Traverse is limited to 20 degrees]*. Owing to its cross-country performance and its armor, it is able to follow anywhere its own infantry or armored troops.

Support for the infantry in attack is the chief mission of the assault gun by virtue of its armor, maneuverability, and cross-country performance and of the rapidity with which it can open fire. The moral support which the infantry receives through its presence is important.

It does not fire on the move. In close fighting it is vulnerable because its sides are light and it is open-topped. Besides, it has no facilities for defending itself at close quarters. As it is not in a position to carry out independent reconnaissance and fighting tasks, this weapon must always be supported by infantry.

In support of an infantry attack, the assault gun engages the enemy heavy infantry weapons which cannot be quickly or effectively destroyed by other weapons. In support of a tank attack, it takes over part of the role of the Pz. Kw. 4, and deals with enemy antitank guns appearing on the front. It will only infrequently be employed as divisional artillery, if the tactical and ammunition situation permits. Assault artillery is not to be included in the divisional artillery fire plan, but is to be treated only as supplementary, and to be used for special tasks (e.g., roving batteries). Its employment for its principal tasks must always be assured.

[The April 1942 document states that "The assault gun may be successfully used against armored vehicles, and light and medium tanks." The May 1940 document, however, states "It is not to be used for antitank purposes, and will only engage enemy tanks in self-defense

or where the antitank guns cannot successfully deal with them." This apparent contradiction can perhaps be explained by the fact that, prior to the invasion of Russia in 1941, this weapon had been used in limited numbers only. Experience on the Eastern Front may have shown that it could be successfully used against tanks, although Russian sources refer to it as essentially an infantry support weapon. A more logical explanation perhaps lies in two German technical developments since 1940: namely, hollow-charge ammunition, which is designed to achieve good armor-piercing performance at relatively low muzzle velocities, and the reported replacement of the short-barreled low-velocity 75-mm with the long-barreled high-velocity tank gun (7.5-cm KwK 40) on some of the newer models.]

b. ORGANIZATION OF THE ASSAULT ARTILLERY BATTALION AND ITS BATTERIES

The assault gun battalion consists of battalion headquarters and three batteries. The battery has six guns—three platoons, each of two guns. *[The April 1942 document states that a battery has 7 guns, the extra gun being "for the battery commander."]* The command vehicles for battery and platoon commanders are armored. They make possible, therefore, movement right up to the foremost infantry line to direct the fire.

c. PRINCIPLES FOR EMPLOYMENT
(1) GENERAL

Assault gun battalions belong to GHQ artillery. For the conduct of certain engagements, battalions or separate batteries are attached to divisions, or to special task forces. The division commander should attach some or all of the assault artillery batteries under his control to infantry or tank units; only in exceptional circumstances will they be put under the artillery commander. Transfer of batteries from support of one unit to another within the division can be carried out very quickly in the course of a battle. Close liaison with the batteries and within the batteries is of primary importance for the timely fulfillment of their missions. The assault artillery fires from positions in open ground, hidden as far as possible from ground and air observation. Only when employed as part of the divisional artillery will these guns fire from covered positions.

Splitting up of assault-gun units into small parts (platoons or single guns) jeopardizes the fire power and facilitates enemy defense. This should occur only in exceptional cases when the entire battalion cannot be employed, i.e., support of special assault troops or employment over terrain which does not permit observation. If employed singly, mutual fire support and mutual assistance in case of breakdowns and over rough country are not possible.

As complete a picture as possible must be obtained of the enemy's armor-piercing weapons and the positions of his mines; hasty employment without sufficient reconnaissance might well jeopardize the attack. Premature deployment must also be avoided. After an engagement, assault guns must not be given security missions, especially at night. They must be withdrawn for refuelling, overhauling, and resupply. After 4 to 5 days in action, they must be thoroughly serviced. If this is not possible, it must be expected that some will not be fit for action and may fall out. When in rear areas, they must be allotted space near repair shops so that they are readily accessible to maintenance facilities, etc.

Troops co-operating with assault guns must give all support possible in dealing with mines and other obstacles. Artillery and heavy infantry weapons must give support by engaging enemy armor-piercing weapons.

Surprise is essential for the successful employment of assault-gun battalions. It is therefore most important for them to move up and into firing positions under cover, and generally to commence fire without warning. Stationary batteries fire on targets which are for the moment most dangerous to the infantry (especially enemy heavy infantry weapons), destroy them, and then withdraw to cover in order to avoid enemy fire. With the allotment of smoke ammunition (23 percent of the total ammunition issue), it is possible to lay smoke and to blind enemy weapons which, for example, are sited on the flank. Assault artillery renders support to tanks usually after the hostile position has been broken into. In this role, assault-gun batteries supplement Pz. Kw. 4s, and during the fluid stages of the battle direct their fire against enemy antitank weapons to the direct front. They follow very closely the first waves of tanks. Destruction of enemy antitank weapons on the flanks of an attack will frequently be the task of the Pz. Kw. 4.

Against concrete positions, assault guns should be used to engage casemates with armor-piercing shells. Co-operation with assault engineers using flame-throwers is very effective in these cases.

Assault guns are only to be used in towns and woods in conjunction with particularly strong and close infantry support, unless the visibility and field of fire are so limited as to make use of the guns impossible without endangering friendly troops. Assault guns are not suitable for use in darkness. Their use in snow is also restricted, as they must usually keep to available roads where enemy defense is sure to be met.

(2) TACTICAL EMPLOYMENT

(A) ON THE MOVE

Vehicles on the move should be kept well spaced. Since the average speed of assault guns is about 15 mph, they must be used in leap-frog fashion when operating with an infantry division. Crossing bridges must be the subject of careful handling. Speed must be reduced to less than 5 mph, and the assault guns must keep exactly to the middle of the bridge, with intervals of at least 35 yards. Bridges must be capable of a load of 22 tons. The commander of the assault guns must cooperate with the officer in charge of the bridge.

(1) In the Infantry Division

While on the move, the division commander keeps the assault-gun battalion as long as possible under his own control. According to the situation and the terrain he can, while on the move, place one assault gun battery in each combat team. The attachment of these weapons to the advance guard is exceptional. In general, assault gun batteries are concentrated in the interval between the advance guard and the main body, and are subject to the orders of the column commander. [According to the April 1942 document, the issue is only 10 percent smoke. It is probable that the ammunition issue depends on the particular operations involved.] On the march, the battery commander and his party should accompany the column commander.

(2) In the Armored Division

On the move, the assault gun battalion attached to an armored division can be used to best advantage if included in the advance guard.

(B) IN THE ATTACK WITH AN INFANTRY DIVISION

The division commander normally attaches assault-gun batteries to the infantry regiments. On receipt of orders placing him under command of an infantry regiment, the battery commander must report in person to the commander of that infantry regiment. Exhaustive discussion between these two (as to enemy situation, preparation of the regiment for the attack, proposed conduct of the attack, main point of the attack, co-operation with divisional artillery, etc.) will provide the basis for the ultimate employment of the assault-gun battery.

It is an error to allot to the battery tasks and targets which can be undertaken by the heavy infantry weapons or the divisional artillery. The battery should rather be employed to engage such nests of resistance as are not known before the beginning of the attack, and which, at the beginning or in the course of the battle, cannot be quickly enough engaged by heavy infantry weapons and artillery. It is the special role of the assault-gun battery to assist the infantry in fighting its way through deep enemy defense zones. Therefore, it must not be committed until the divisional artillery and the heavy infantry weapons can no longer render adequate support.

The attached battery can be employed as follows:

(1) Before the attack begins, it is located so as to be capable of promptly supporting the regiment's main effort; (or)

(2) The battery is held in the rear, and is only committed if, after the attack begins, a clear picture is obtained of the enemy's dispositions.

Under both circumstances the attachment of the battery, and occasionally of individual platoons, to a battalion may be advantageous.

The commander under whose command the battery is placed gives the battery commander his orders. The latter makes clear to his platoon commanders the specific battle tasks, and shows them, as far as possible on the ground, the targets to be engaged. When in action the battery commander, together with his platoon commanders, must at all times be familiar with the hostile situation, and must reconnoiter the ground over which he is to move and attack. The battery will be so disposed by the platoon commanders in the sectors in which it is expected later to operate that, as it approaches the enemy, the battery, under cover, can follow the infantry from sector to sector. How distant an objective can be given, and yet permit the control of fire by the battery and platoon commanders, is dependent on the country, enemy strength, and enemy action. In close country, and when the enemy weapons are well camouflaged, targets cannot be given to the platoons by the battery commander. In these circumstances, fire control falls to the platoon commanders. The platoons must then co-operate constantly with the most advanced infantry platoons; they remain close to the infantry and engage the nearest targets. The question of dividing a platoon arises only if individual guns are allotted to infantry companies or platoons to carry out specific tasks: e.g., for action deep into the enemy's battle position.

In an attack by tanks attached to an infantry division, the assault-artillery battalion engages chiefly enemy antitank weapons. In this case too, the assault-gun battalion is attached to infantry elements. Well before the beginning of the tank attack, the batteries are disposed in positions of observation from which they can readily engage enemy antitank weapons. They follow up the tanks by platoons, and under special conditions—e.g., in unreconnoitered country— by guns, as soon as possible. In a deep attack, co-operation with tanks leading an infantry attack is possible when the hostile islands of resistance have been disposed of.

In the enemy tank counterattack, our own antitank guns first engage the hostile tanks. The assault-gun battalion engages the enemy heavy weapons which are supporting the enemy tank counterattack. Only when the antitank guns prove insufficient, do assault guns engage enemy tanks. In this case the assault guns advance within effective range of the enemy tanks, halt, and destroy them with antitank shells.

(C) IN THE ATTACK WITH AN ARMORED DIVISION

In such an attack, the following tasks can be carried out by the assault gun battalion:

(1) Support of the tank attack by neutralizing enemy antitank weapons; (and/or)

(2) Support of the attack by motorized infantry elements.

According to the situation and the plan of attack, the battalion, complete or in part, is attached to the armored brigade, sometimes with parts attached also to the motorized infantry brigade. Within the armored brigade, further allotment to tank regiments is normally necessary. As a rule, complete batteries are attached.

To support the initial phase of the tank attack, assault-gun batteries can be placed in positions of observation if suitable ground is already in our possession. Otherwise the batteries follow in the attack close behind the first waves of tanks, and as soon as the enemy is engaged, support the tanks by attacking enemy antitank weapons.

As the tank attack progresses, it is most important to put enemy defensive weapons out of action as soon as possible. Close support of the leading tanks is the main essential to the carrying out of these tasks.

The support of the motorized infantry attack is carried out according to the principles for the support of the foot infantry attack.

(D) IN THE ATTACK AS DIVISIONAL ARTILLERY

In the attack of a division, the employment of the assault gun battalion as part of the divisional artillery is exceptional. In this role, the assault-gun batteries must be kept free for their more usual mission at all times, and must enter battle with a full issue of ammunition.

(E) IN THE PURSUIT

In the pursuit, assault-gun batteries should be close to their own infantry in order to break at once any enemy resistance. Very close support of the leading infantry units increases their forward momentum. Temporary allotment of individual platoons—under exceptional circumstances, of individual guns—is possible.

(F) IN THE DEFENSE

In the defense, the primary task of assault artillery is the support of counterthrusts and counterattacks. The assembly area must be sufficiently far from the friendly battle position to enable the assault-gun units to move speedily to that sector which is threatened with a breakthrough. Allotment and employment are carried out according to the plan of the infantry attack. The point of commitment should be arranged as early as possible with the commanders of the infantry units allocated to the counterthrust or counterattack. In the defense as in the attack, the assault-artillery battalion will only be employed in an antitank role if it must defend itself against a tank attack. (Only 12 percent of the ammunition issue is armor-piercing.) [15 percent according to the April 1942 document.] If employed as part of the divisional artillery (which is rare), the battalion will be placed under the division artillery commander.

(G) IN THE WITHDRAWAL

For the support of infantry in withdrawal, batteries, and even individual platoons or guns, are allotted to infantry units. By virtue of their armor, assault guns are able to engage enemy targets even when the infantry has already withdrawn. To assist disengagement from the enemy, tank attacks carried out with limited objectives can be supported by assault guns. Allotment of assault-gun batteries or platoons to rear parties or rear guards is effective.

d. SUPPLIES

As GHQ troops, the battalion takes with it its complete initial issue of ammunition, fuel, and rations. When it is attached to a division, its further supply is handled by the division. The battalion commander is responsible for the correct supply of the battalion and the individual batteries, especially in the pursuit. Every battery, platoon, and gun commander must constantly have in mind the supply situation of his unit. It is his duty to report his needs in sufficient time and with foresight, and to take the necessary action to replenish depleted supplies of ammunition, fuel, and rations.

32. NOTES ON SOME GERMAN TACTICS USED IN RUSSIA

Tactical and Technical Trends, No. 20, March 11th 1942

Reports from an Allied Mission attached to the Russian Army highlights some tactical maneuvers used by the Germans in the Russian operations. Some of these tactics are mentioned under the following headings:

a. General Characteristics

The close cooperation of all arms was brought into play—all arms being subordinated to the success of mass tank formations. Great stress was laid on speed and surprise. Though detailed orders were issued, full scope was allowed to local commanders for their execution.

b. Surprise

Surprise was achieved by secrecy, rumors, and false orders. Tanks were moved about (especially by rail) in an area where the main blow was not to take place, and at the same time, the main striking force was kept concealed elsewhere. Immobile dummy tanks were also used.

c. Psychological Methods

At the moment of a tank attack, paratroops armed with automatic weapons were dropped. Troops which had gotten to the rear of the Russian defenses fired indiscriminately in an attempt to break the defenders' morale. Parachutists or motorcyclists were used for the seizure of nerve centers.

d. Frontal Attacks

Frontal attacks were always avoided by the Germans. German tanks reacted quickly to antitank fire; where a strong antitank defense was met the attack at that point would be called off. The Germans then would appear to be getting ready for a second attack in the same place, but would in fact be searching the front for spots that were weak in antitank defense.

e. Advance

While the leading detachments proceeded forward, the German main body would follow in march column. When resistance is encountered, the leading detachments deploy on a wide front, and strong reconnaissance detachments are sent out to the flanks; the main body remains in march column.

f. Attack

The arrowhead formation was the normal form of attack used. The order of march was as follows:

(1) Motorcyclists, with assault weapons in the lead;
(2) Tank regiment, with two battalions forward if frontage is 1 to 2 miles;
(3) Armored infantry, deeply echeloned.

The remaining infantry either advanced far to one flank or remained concentrated in the center ready to widen any gap that presented itself.

g. Defense

The defense was very elastic. Towards dusk, detachments of armored infantry would move forward in front of the main line of resistance to give the impression that the edge of the defensive zone was further forward than it actually was. The remainder prepared the main battle position. Some tanks were dug in on the defensive position. When the defensive preparations were completed, a majority of the tanks withdrew to assembly points in the rear. A few single Pz.Kw. 3's and 4's remained dug in on the position as pivots of fire.

There follow Russian answers to questions concerning the tactics and operation of German armor in the Russian campaign.

(1) Where do the various German Headquarters march in a full-scale tank attack?

During battle, the Headquarters of a tank force is placed as near as possible to the forward units, in order to obtain observation over the field of battle. Protection of communications with flank and rear units from fire is one of the considerations affecting the location of the command post.

(2) What is known about protection of tanks on the march and in final assembly positions?

Assembly positions and routes of advance are usually protected by three tiers of fighter planes flying at heights of from 18,000 to 20,000 feet, the most intensive patrolling being at 6,000 to 7,500 feet.

(3) Describe aircraft support during a tank breakthrough.

The tank attack is preceded by attacks by bomber aircraft (Ju-87, Ju-88, less frequently He-111) and by fighters (Me-110), in groups of from 20 to 30 planes endeavoring to pave the way for the tanks. The Me-110's operate in front of the bombers, attacking enemy troops with their cannon and machine guns.

When organizing cooperation between aircraft and tanks, the German command pays a great deal of attention to communications and control. Therefore, an air force control post is established with each Armored Division. These posts are commanded by experienced air force officers, who ride in the tank unit commander's tank at the head of the column. In contact by radio with the air force control post, he directs the aircraft to the targets as required.

(4) How are fuel and ammunition supplied to tank units which have broken through to the rear of the enemy?

The German command employs transport aircraft (preferably Ju-52) to supply such tank units as have broken through into the rear of the enemy defenses with ammunition and fuel. The Germans have a considerable number of transport aircraft and provide substantial help to small groups of tanks. But the basic problem of supplying tank units with fuel and ammunition devolves upon line-of-communications organizations.

In so far as the cooperation of the German air force with tanks is concerned, there is a marked tendency on the part of the German command to employ their air force with great mobility. In the course of operations in the south of Russia, it was noticed that the German air force units were rapidly moved from one sector of the front to another, as operations required.

33. GERMAN ANTITANK UNITS AND TACTICS

Tactical and Technical Trends, No. 10, October 22nd 1942

EQUIPMENT

Successful offensive and defensive action against mechanized forces demands specialized equipment. The principal weapons employed by the Germans against opposing armor are guns of various calibers, mines, obstacles, and grenades. This materiel has been developed over a period of several years and has withstood the test of combat.

A list of the standard German antitank guns has been given in Tactical and Technical Trends, No. 5, p. 9.

An obstacle is any object or device capable of halting a tank or of impeding its progress. Some of the more common forms of obstacles used by the Germans are minefields, road blocks, antitank ditches, and concrete barriers. Obstacles are also constructed from damaged vehicles, trees cut and placed across an avenue of approach, explosive charges which make craters in a roadway, coils of wire disposed in depth to foul the tracks of tanks, and mines suspended from the branches of trees. Antipersonnel mines and booby traps are often used to make obstacles more difficult to remove. Obstacles and barriers are habitually covered with fire to insure their continued effectiveness.

The pole charge consists of a small explosive charge attached to the end of a fairly long pole. The most effective explosive used by the Germans for this purpose is a prepared demolition called the Pionier-Sprengbüchse. It contains slightly more than 2 pounds of explosive and can disable most tanks. Other kinds of explosives are used in makeshift pole charges with almost equal effectiveness.

The "Molotov cocktail," which proved its effectiveness during the Spanish Civil War, has been adopted and used by the German Army. It consists in essence of a quart bottle of gasoline with a gasoline-soaked rag attached to its base. The infantryman lights the rag and throws the bottle at the tank. When the bottle breaks, the tank is immediately engulfed in flame. Improved models of this bomb have been used in which the gasoline is ignited by a substance which explodes on contact with a hard surface. The bottle is sometimes filled with smoke-producing materials to blind the tank crew or with slow-burning combustible oils.

The stick or "potato-masher" grenade (M24) normally contains 1 1/4 pounds of explosive and has a 5 1/2-second time fuze. For use against tanks, the heads of five or six grenades are tied in a bunch around a seventh.

The grenade PH 39 is newer than the M24 and is said to have from six to eight times greater effect. It contains 1 5/16 pounds of explosive and has a 4 1/2 second time fuze. One of these grenades is usually sufficient to put a light or medium tank out of action if it strikes a vital spot.

ORGANIZATION

Small antitank units such as the platoon and company are organic parts of larger organizations (regiments and battalions), and their mission is to provide these organizations with defense from armored attack. Large antitank units such as battalions and GHQ forces are used as general reserves, and either allotted according to the requirements of lower units or committed at critical points during an action. Normally, the antitank units which are employed as reserve forces are given a large number of sell-propelled guns to provide the mobility essential to their missions.

Flexibility, which is a characteristic of all German organization, is especially apparent in the makeup of antitank units. This is partly because antimechanized forces are employed in support of other arms and change their composition according to the task, and partly because of the shift from 37-mm to 50-mm AT guns. As units have their armament and number of guns changed, they have a corresponding change in personnel and services.

At present it is difficult to say with any exactness what type of guns any given antitank unit will have. Weapons are issued to units from the available supply, and the newer types are being allotted as rapidly as they are produced. The unit organizations given below are standard, but not necessarily the only types which the German Army will employ.

The GHQ reserve pool contains heavy antitank battalions, antitank battalions, and probably some self-propelled tank-hunter battalions.

The infantry division's antitank units include one antitank battalion; in addition, each of its three infantry regiments has an antitank company.

The armored division has one antitank battalion, in addition, in each heavy weapons company of its reconnaissance battalion, motorcycle battalion, and two motorized rifle regiments, there is an antitank platoon.

Both the mountain division and the motorized infantry division each have one antitank battalion. The latter also may have one tank-hunter battalion for each of its three motorized rifle regiments.

COMPOSITION OF ANTITANK UNITS

The antitank battalion comprises headquarters and staff; three companies, each with four 37-mm AT guns, six 50-mm AT guns, six machine guns, organic transportation, and a maintenance section; and a signal section with 6 pack radios, 2 armored radios, and a lineman's section.

Arms carried in the antitank battalion are twelve 37-mm AT guns, eighteen 50-mm AT guns, 18 machine guns, 315 rifles, 204 pistols, and 13 machine pistols (submachine guns). Accompanying the guns at all times are 180 rounds of 37-mm ammunition per gun, 38 to 72 rounds of 50-mm ammunition per gun, and 1,000 rounds of machine-gun ammunition per gun.

The heavy antitank battalion is a GHQ unit made up of 88-mm and 50-mm guns. Its exact composition is not known, but is believed to vary widely according to the number of weapons available.

The tank-hunter battalion contains two companies of 47-mm antitank guns on self-propelled mounts (Mark I tank chassis), or as a variation, one company of 47-mm AT guns and one company of 37-mm AT guns. These tank-destroyer units may also be organized as GHQ troops.

The antitank company of an infantry regiment is fully mechanized, and consists of headquarters and four platoons. Each of the platoons consists of three sections, each armed with a 37-mm AT gun, and one light machine-gun section. Some 50-mm guns have replaced the 37-mm guns which have formerly made up this company's armament.

The antitank platoon of the heavy weapons company is thought to be the same as a platoon of an infantry antitank company.

Barrier detachments are not part of the antitank forces, but their approximate makeup is given here because of their important tactical mission of constructing antimechanized obstacles. Since barrier detachments are engineer task forces constituted for specific missions, no definite organization exists. A typical barrier detachment (Sperr Abteilung) for a corps would comprise an engineer battalion; a mechanized column (Sperr Kollone) equipped with explosives; one or more bicycle companies; one or more battalions of artillery; and a signal platoon. Such a unit organized to assist division antitank forces would include the following: The division engineer battalion (or part of it); elements of the antitank battalion; one or more bicycle companies; one or more batteries of artillery; and some infantry elements.

All of these forces are supplied with large numbers of motor vehicles, giving them the increased mobility necessary for the rapid performance of their tasks.

TRAINING

When entering the German military service all soldiers take a basic training course of 6 weeks prior to being assigned to permanent units. For the men of antitank units, this period consists of: intensive training in basic infantry subjects; recognition of enemy and friendly armored vehicles; laying and firing antitank weapons and small arms; and handling antitank vehicles and guns. Along with their technical training, they learn something of the theory of the employment of antitank forces and get a course of physical toughening.

In addition to these basic training courses, there are courses designed to make soldiers antitank specialists. A document captured from a German prisoner in Libya gives a good idea of the content of such a course. A translation of his account follows:

"The course lasted from 8 to 10 weeks. During the mornings of the first 2 weeks, we learned the principles of gun laying and aiming, with considerable practice in aiming at the 'snake' target, which is 10 feet high and placed at a distance of 35 feet. The gun must be brought into position and correct aim taken in 60 seconds. The snake target can be given both vertical and horizontal movement.

"The afternoons were spent in manhandling the gun at double time. The 37-mm gun was drawn by two men with ropes, with two men pushing behind. Each gun had a commander. After every 20 minutes there was a 10-minute break. The whole distance to be covered was about 5 miles. The last stretch of more than 2 miles rose about 330 feet and included several hollows. This distance was crosscountry and had to be covered in an hour. On arrival at the top of the hill there was a further 10-minute break which was followed by training in judging distances to farmhouses, trees, etc. The distances were checked and corrected with a rangefinder.

"Aiming and firing with dummy cartridges were then practiced on moving targets of cars camouflaged as tanks. These cars moved at the same speed as tanks. They were at ranges of from 450 to 1,350 yards and in a field of vision 350 yards wide. During this practice the gun positions were moved as much as 100 yards.

"The return journey, mostly downhill, had to be covered in 70 minutes. For the last 10 minutes before arrival at barracks, the crews marched along, ropes over their shoulders, singing lustily. The whole exercise was carried out in full kit—steel helmet, rifle, gas mask, pack canteen, and cartridge belts filled with old iron.

"Fifteen minutes was allowed for changing into fatigue clothes; then followed a 30-minute period of instruction in gun cleaning, followed by theoretical instruction in gun parts.

"The third, fourth, and fifth weeks were spent mainly in theoretical instruction and firing practice with a detachable sub-caliber barrel liner. Ammunition fired was the same as used in the service rifle, and the range was about 10 yards. The size of the figures on the target was about 2 inches square. On the targets were four squares, each with five figures, which were fired upon in any order in accordance with the instructions of the gun leader. The time allowed for sighting, loading, and firing was 35 seconds, and the standard to be attained was four hits and one near miss. In addition, there was 45 minutes daily of double-time gun drill in which turning, stopping, crosscountry movement, and getting the weapon into firing position were practiced.

"The remainder of the course included further gun drill—laying, sighting, and loading with dummy cartridges. All of the exercises were aimed at inculcating speed. The first gun set the pace and the other three guns had to keep up with it. Toward the end of the course there was some field firing. For snap shooting, each gunner was allowed five rounds.

"Wooden practice tanks of the same size as normal tanks were pulled along at a speed of 6 miles per hour. These practice tanks were suspended from overhead ropes, and rollers were used to make them turn corners. The five rounds were to be fired at 1,350, 1,100, 880, 660, and 440 yards, respectively. The qualifying score was 80 percent. Afterwards, there was firing practice at cardboard figures representing machine-gun nests. These figures were life-sized, and represented the personnel as either prone or kneeling. The qualifying score in this exercise was 100 percent. Five rounds were fired on this range, one at 440 yards, one at 660, and the other three at 880. Gunners who made the best records were rewarded by being allowed to fire 10 extra rounds.

"Instruction both practical and theoretical, was also given in fighting British incendiary bombs and land mines. There were occasionally exercises with rubber boats, in which the antitank guns were to be transported across rivers. At the end of the period of training there were maneuvers for 3 days."

After his preliminary work, the German antitank soldier goes into unit training. The primary objective of unit training in the German Army is teamwork. Since soldiers come to antitank companies and battalions with a good knowledge of their weapons, the first lesson that they learn is the employment of these weapons in a closely coordinated team. Most of this instruction is by platoons, as the platoon is the antitank unit most frequently used in actual combat.

A great deal of the instruction is in the movement and emplacement of the guns, and gun crews are taught rapid and effective means of selecting and camouflaging positions. Gunnery, however, is not neglected, for there is frequent practice in laying and firing weapons. As in the basic courses, great stress is laid on the manhandling of guns, and there are frequent company and platoon exercises in which guns are put into position, moved to new positions, and fired without the use of prime movers.

Officers of antitank units are trained to exercise a great amount of initiative in the disposition of their guns and in coping with unexpected conditions. Speed in making decisions is emphasized.

TACTICAL EMPLOYMENT OF ANTIMECHANIZED UNITS

As German pre-war military philosophy worked out a theory of combat emphasizing movement, armor, and air support, one fact became apparent: the development of the armored and air arms had swung the balance of power in battle heavily in favor of the offense. More specifically, the Germans calculated that each antitank gun attacked by compact tank units could hardly destroy more than three tanks before being submerged by the advance. On this basis, they decided that to reestablish the equality between attack and defense it would be necessary to protect antitank weapons effectively by camouflage, concealment, and armor, and to oppose tank attacks with a flexible and mobile mass of guns on self-propelled mounts, capable of strengthening defense in depth.

Another development in the theory of antimechanized tactics, the offensive attitude, has been equally important in the evolution of the present German system. With the development of a large number of mobile guns, giving antimechanized units more mobility than tanks, it was realized that guns need no longer lie in wait for the armored attack, but could seek combat with enemy armored vehicles. Every soldier was impressed with the ability of new weapons and methods to destroy tanks, and the names of units were changed from Panzerabwehr (antitank defense) to Panzerjäger (tank hunter). (It is interesting to compare this German change in attitude with a similar change in the U.S. Army, where "antitank" battalions have been changed to "tank destroyer" battalions and the offensive character of antimechanized operations emphasized.)

A captured German training manual emphasizes the offensive role of the division antitank battalion and the GHQ antitank units, saying:

"As a result of its speed, mobility, crosscountry performance, and protection against tanks, the antitank battalion can attack enemy armored vehicles. Its object is to engage and destroy enemy tanks by surprise attacks from unexpected directions with concentrated fire. In addition to engaging enemy tanks, the antitank unit has the task of neutralizing antitank defenses, thereby supporting its own tanks."

The only real protective missions which are now assigned to antimechanized units are those of the antitank companies of infantry regiments and the antitank platoons of heavy weapons companies. Division antitank battalions and GHQ antitank units are always considered as reserve forces or as offensive elements. The organic companies are used for local protection, but are not expected to repel tank attacks in force; for this purpose the more mobile battalions are committed at the point where the main force of the armored attack strikes.

The actual proportion of self-propelled guns in the German Army at present is not known, but it is believed that the objective is for all GHQ units to be self-propelled throughout, and for division antitank battalions and regimental antitank companies to be two-thirds self-propelled. This would provide a high degree of mobility, while retaining a few easily camouflaged towed guns, which could be used well forward to protect avenues of tank attack.

In battle, emphasis is place on antitank units moving rapidly in and out of position. All of the personnel and installations of antitank units are required to be prepared for tank attack at all times. Careful and continuous reconnaissance is deemed a necessity, as each unit must be familiar with the most likely routes of tank approach and be prepared to defend these routes.

Special emphasis is laid on reports by all subordinate units on the approach of tanks. These reports, combined with the reports of reconnaissance agencies, permit the timely and coordinated organization of defensive measures.

The antitank battalion of an armored division goes into the attack with the tanks, following them from objective to objective, and engages all tanks threatening them from the flanks and rear. Some detachments of the antitank battalion may also be allotted to the infantry following the tanks if this is necessary for security.

If infantry is attacking without tanks, the antitank battalion accompanies it in the same manner as when accompanying the tank attack, except that the main body of the battalion is kept behind the infantry flanks to repulse enemy counterattacks or overcome unexpectedly strong enemy resistance. Units of the antitank battalion are not usually attached to larger units of the attacking force, but furnish independent support.

Platoon commanders are instructed to display a great amount of initiative in engaging targets. If there are no enemy armored vehicles encountered on one platoon sector, the platoon gives necessary assistance to the guns of neighboring sectors. Camouflage of guns in successive attack positions is not required, but platoon leaders are cautioned to use the greatest care in the proper selection of positions which command important terrain.

In a pursuit, antitank units are attached to the most advanced elements, usually by platoons. They have the mission of giving protection to the flanks of the most advanced elements and of destroying armored elements in the enemy rearguard, thus breaking the backbone of the enemy delaying action.

In a withdrawal, regimental antitank units normally defend their regimental units along the line of advance of enemy tanks. Part of the division antitank battalion may be used to strengthen this defense. In the case of an exterior division or of a division operating alone, some of the antitank battalion may be employed for the protection of flanks.

The remainder of the division antitank battalion is divided into two parts. One reconnoiters and prepares positions for the next delaying action, while the other acts as a mobile reserve for the immediate use of the division commander.

In spite of the offensive emphasis given to the antitank units of the German Army, their primary mission remains defensive. In performing this defensive mission, however, these units may use some of their offensive tactics with great success.

The terrain plays an important part in plans for the defense of a sector against mechanized attack. After thorough reconnaissance of the defensive sector assigned to a division, the plan for antitank defense is perfected. The principles of this plan are, generally, to deny the best avenues of tank approach to the enemy by covering them with liberal antitank fire, while the less likely avenues of approach are denied to the enemy by obstacles. The antitank units organic in regiments are used well to the front and are emplaced in camouflaged positions; the division antitank battalion on its mobile mounts is kept in the rear, ready to lend support where needed and to give depth to the defense.

Typical German procedure for the preparation of antitank defense in a defensive situation is as follows *[This account is based on a problem given at the Kriegsakademie, the German equivalent of the U.S. Command and General Staff School.]*:

(a) Assume that the division is defending a sector 9,000 yards wide, regiments abreast. The terrain is diversified, offering some tank obstacles, such as canals, thick woods, and a stream, and also offering open, rolling corridors which are excellent avenues of approach for tanks.

(b) Reconnaissance and map study are made to determine two important locations along the front: one, the engineer center of resistance (Pionier Schwerpunkt) and the other, the antitank-gun center of resistance (Panzer Abwehrgeschutz Schwerpunkt).

(c) The engineer center of resistance is located in that section of the front where natural obstacles contribute defensive strength. Engineer troops improve and expand the natural defensive features found in this section.

(d) The antitank-gun center of resistance is located in that section of the front where the ground is open and rolling, ideal terrain for tank operations. The regimental antitank company's guns are emplaced in concealed positions 200 to 400 yards in rear of the main line of resistance, while the antitank battalion is farther to the rear, with gun positions echeloned in depth. The battalion gun positions are selected, and positions leading thereto carefully reconnoitered, but they are not usually occupied until the warning of a hostile attack is received. The guns remain under cover in positions of readiness, conveniently located to permit rapid movement to any threatened area.

Antitank defense on the march follows the same general principles as in a static situation—that is, the regimental antitank companies provide defense for their units, and the division antitank battalion acts as a general reserve to be used against a concentrated tank attack.

Within the regimental march column, the antitank company is employed in units of full platoons. The four platoons are usually disposed as follows: one platoon has one gun with the point and the

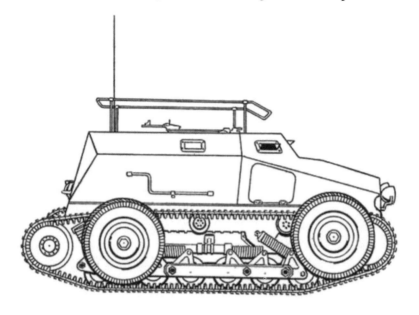

remaining two guns at the rear of the advance party; one platoon is placed at the head and one at the rear of the reserve; and the last platoon marches with the combat trains. If, however, the regiment is marching in the division's main body, one platoon marches at the head of the regiment, one at the rear of the foot elements, and the other two platoons with the combat trains.

The location of the division on the march is the determining factor in the disposition of the division antitank battalion. When the division has both flanks covered, the battalion marches with the combat trains; when there is an exposed flank and a strong tank attack is possible, the battalion protects the exposed flank, moving from position to position by bounds, the companies leap-frogging each other so that two companies are always in position to fire.

The division commander determines the tank-warning system prior to the start of the march, reconnaissance elements being marshalled to insure early intelligence of the approach of hostile armored elements.

OBSTACLES AND MINES

German engineers cooperate closely with antimechanized units in defense against tanks. As previously stated, engineers reinforce by obstacles and mines the terrain less favorable for tank attack, whereas the antitank guns are massed in those areas not easily defended by artificial barriers. Both obstacles and minefields are always covered by the fire of antitank weapons and small arms. As a matter of fact, the Germans often use these antimechanized obstacles to slow or halt tanks and make them good targets.

The Germans make every effort to slow or halt pursuing hostile forces by mining roads and bridges. Mines are buried under the earth or in snow, and may often be detected by the presence of small mounds.

The Germans employ antitank minefields extensively, finding them particularly valuable in the desert, where flat terrain and hard soil makes the construction of artificial obstacles quite difficult. These fields are often laid in complicated patterns. As a result their removal is difficult and hazardous, since the uncovering of a small portion of the field usually does not give the key to the remainder. The hazard of clearing these fields is increased by the liberal use of antipersonnel mines scattered among the antitank mines.

German minefields are usually very plainly marked, to warn friendly vehicles. The Germans consider safety in this respect more important than deception. In the rear areas they often string a low wire fence around the fields, or dig a shallow ditch. In some cases guards are placed at the gaps in the minefields to see friendly vehicles through safely.

Minefields are employed with great care, as the Germans appreciate that it is possible for them to be turned to the disadvantage of the unit that lays them. The object is to construct an obstacle that will block enemy vehicles without hampering the maneuver of German forces.

Antimechanized obstacles are built by special engineer task forces (Sperrabteilung) who must have great mobility. Their personnel is taught the necessity for the rapid performance of their jobs.

The cardinal principle of the location of antimechanized barriers is that they are placed in such a manner as to cause tanks and other vehicles to appear at practically point-blank range in fields of fire of the weapons covering them.

USE OF ANTIAIRCRAFT AGAINST TANKS

In the German Army it is emphasized that antiaircraft and antitank guns have the same general characteristics—high muzzle velocity, mobility, wide traverse, and rapid rate of fire—and therefore antiaircraft guns should be used to assist in defense against tank attack. This role is generally regarded as secondary, but on occasion part of the German antiaircraft weapons have been employed against armor during a simultaneous air and tank attack. In some cases antiaircraft units have been assigned to higher units with the primary mission of furnishing additional antitank protection.

INFANTRY TANK HUNTING

German training and operations have both emphasized the

importance of aggressive action against tanks by dismounted infantry personnel. All tanks, they teach, have certain vulnerable points which make them easy prey for close-combat weapons specially designed for the purpose and employed by aggressive, trained soldiers. The chief weaknesses of tanks are their relatively poor visibility, their inability to defend themselves within a close radius of the vehicle (dead space), and the time lag in shifting guns from target to target. They also need certain times, usually at night or in rear areas, to carry out maintenance and repairs. This is always a favorable time for the dismounted tank hunter.

Tank hunters, acting alone or in pairs, are also taught to use smoke candles, smoke grenades, and smudges to produce films on the vision slits of the tanks. By using these methods they can get within close enough range to employ hand weapons.

A German training instruction, issued to an infantry unit shortly after it had successfully repelled a British attack, sets forth the basic technique of infantry tank hunting. A translation of the document follows:

"The construction of our defensive areas has proved extremely effective, particularly the provision of antitank trenches. No casualties were sustained when British armored fighting vehicles penetrated our position. The troops were protected by antitank trenches and could employ their weapons on the infantry following the tanks, while the tanks were being engaged by antitank weapons.

"The lesson to be drawn is that the infantryman should allow the tank to pass overhead while he is in his antitank trench. If he attempts to jump clear, he draws fire on himself from the tank, whose field of fire is extremely limited. The infantryman's main task remains the repulsing of the assaulting infantry. In addition to this, however, enemy tanks can be knocked out by courageous action with close-combat weapons.

"The most important weapons for this purpose are the Molotov cocktail and the pole charge. The most convenient charge is the prepared charge (Pionier Sprengbüchse), which contains 2.2 pounds of explosive. Its strength is such that it can knock out a British infantry tank without unduly endangering its user by the explosion. The drag-mine is also highly successful.

"Molotov cocktails are most effective if they burst on the ribs of the engine cover. The flaming contents envelop the motor, which is usually set afire.

"The tank is particularly sensitive to the prepared charge in three places—on the tracks, the engine cover, and the horizontal armor near the turret. If a prepared charge bursts in close proximity to the tracks, the chain is damaged to such an extent that it breaks when the tank moves forward. A charge placed on the reinforcing ribs penetrates them and the engine cover, damaging the engine. The horizontal armor near the turret is weak in the English infantry tank, and the detonation of a charge there causes complete penetration and great blast effect within the tank. The drag mine can be effectively used by an infantryman in his antitank trench.

"In order to employ the close-combat weapons mentioned above, the infantryman must at least be within throwing range of the tank. He must, therefore, wait in his cover for the tank to approach. But this cover is useful only when it has been specifically constructed as an antitank ditch—that is, it must be level with the ground, well camouflaged, and not more than 40 inches wide, so that the tank can pass overhead without endangering the infantryman.

"The danger to the infantryman who finds himself close to a tank is slight. An infantryman in his antitank trench is always superior to an enemy tank that is within throwing range if he is properly equipped. The periscope of the British tanks is inadequate, allowing the driver to see straight ahead only, and the gunner can only see in the line of his gun. Because of the limited play of the weapons' mountings, they cannot be depressed sufficiently to cover the immediate vicinity of the tank. An infantryman in this dead area must inevitably use his close-combat weapons effectively."

34. GERMAN LIGHT ARMORED OP VEHICLE

Tactical and Technical Trends,
No. 11, November 5th 1942

A description has been received of a light armored OP vehicle (Sd Kfz 259) mounted on a wheel-and-track suspension. (See accompanying sketch.)

The four wheels can be raised or lowered by means of arms, so that the vehicle may run on its tracks over rough ground, or on its wheels along roads. Front, side, and rear plates are sloped to the vertical, while the top is horizontal. An observation hatch is fitted in the roof; slit openings, together with slit opening flaps, are located in the sides and front. A door is fitted in the back for the crew, while a small door, probably for the driver, is to be found on the right side.

Radio is fitted for communication with the gun positions, but there is no evidence of armament or optical instruments, although it has been reported that a BC scope is fitted. This instrument has an azimuth scale.

There is a crew of five, believed to consist of a battery commander, radio operator, observer, chauffeur, and one NCO.

35. USE OF 20-MM AA/AT GUN AGAINST GROUND TARGETS

Intelligence Bulletin, February 1943

1. INTRODUCTION

A German document, evidently written by a platoon commander of an antiaircraft-antitank company, deals with an antiaircraft-antitank battalion's use of the 20-mm dual-purpose gun against ground targets.

2. EXTRACTS FROM THE DOCUMENT

a. General

The 20-mm gun on a self-propelled mount combines the fire power and mobility of an antiaircraft gun with the accuracy and penetration of an antitank gun. It is insufficiently armored, however, and this fault must be offset by making good use of cover and by fire control.

The smallest unit in battle is the section of two guns. Use of single guns, except for individual tasks like the engagement of enemy observation posts, is exceptional. Ground observation is most important; every spare man must be employed on it, and must be made personally ambitious to spot targets.

b. Action During Assembly

During assembly, antiaircraft-antitank troops usually take over protection against air and land attack. Guns must be sited so that attacking aircraft can be engaged from reverse slopes, while, moving the gun to a position on the forward slope, it is possible to bring under fire the enemy approaching on the ground.

c. Action During Attack

The antiaircraft-antitank troops support the advance of the infantry and other arms. For this purpose the antiaircraft-antitank guns should be sited to a flank, to exploit their range fully without endangering the advancing German troops. The addition of 100 yards, more or less, to a flank hardly interferes with the effectiveness of the 20-mm gun, whereas it does affect the enemy's infantry weapons by widening the target.

When in action only the following remain on the vehicle: driver and gun commander and Nos. 1 and 4.[1] When the gun commander is away on reconnaissance for a new gun position, No. 3 takes his place. The other men (who are the ammunition handlers) give protection and carry out flank observation. If there is no mine-spotting section available, the ammunition handlers must search for mines in the ground to be passed over.

The platoon or section commander and his runners follow directly in the rear of the attacking infantry or the assaulting engineer detachment. The commander reconnoiters good positions and good targets for the guns.

d. Fire

Good fire discipline (including good observation) is of the greatest value; this is gained by experience and will be made easier by cooperation with the attacking troops and the various observation posts. The sectors of fire must be assigned. Telescopes and rangefinders will be used to the fullest.

e. Movement

Changes of position must be made quickly. Occupation of a gun position from a flank must be avoided if possible. The guns will advance by bounds. If they meet slight opposition which can be broken by one section, the other section remains in reserve and, after the action, leapfrogs forward as an advance section while the first makes itself ready again.

When close to the enemy—for example, when breaking into his positions—the guns fire on the move. This forces the enemy to take cover, and weakens his morale.

f. Defense

When bivouacking or holding a defensive position, the guns occupy prepared positions under cover. Other alternative positions are prepared, battle outposts are put out, and landmarks are recorded.

g. On the March

On the march the battalion is disposed as follows:

- No. 1 gun—protection to front and right.
- No. 2 gun—protection to front and left.
- No. 3 gun—protection to rear and right.
- No. 4 gun—protection to rear and left.

Under air attack, a similar formation will be adopted. On the section commander's orders, the troops will halt and open fire. Aircraft will be engaged only if they spot or attack the battalion's own positions, if bridges or observation posts need protection, or if the aircraft offer especially good targets.

h. Tanks

It has been proved that the gun, rightly used, can put even the heaviest tanks to flight even if it cannot put them out of action; that is, by its high rate of fire it can jam turrets and gun mantlets. The most effective range against tanks is under 400 yards. Every effort must be made to attack them from the sides.

3. EXTRACT FROM A GERMAN NEWSPAPER'S COMMENT ON THE 20-MM GUN

The duties of the antiaircraft-antitank battalions are, above all, to protect other units against low-flying attacks while on the march and in action. For this purpose the 20-mm gun is principally used.

The battalions are part of the infantry's support. Troops of these units are therefore trained as infantrymen; but, in addition, they learn their own weapons, including training with different sizes of rangefinders in height estimation. Otherwise, the training corresponds to that of flak units. The antiaircraft-antitank units (the platoon is the normal fighting unit) are located in the column of march according to the prearranged operation order. In case of surprise attack, fire is opened either immediately from the tractor on which the gun is mounted, or else sections (which are fully motorized) leave the column and occupy a position on firm ground with a good field of fire, with the gun dismounted. After fighting, the units catch up with their original position in the line of march.

Antiaircraft-antitank guns use only tracer ammunition—high explosive against aircraft, and, if necessary, armor-piercing ammunition against ground targets; they have a limited ceiling and are used principally by day. Antiaircraft-antitank troops have no listening apparatus or searchlight batteries and do not pretend to rival the flak artillery. Further tasks include: protection of divisional artillery against low-flying attack, participation in ground fighting by neutralizing enemy machine-gun nests and other strong points, or defense against single tanks.

More from the same series

Most books from the 'Eastern Front from Primary Sources' series are edited and endorsed by Emmy Award winning film maker and military historian Bob Carruthers, producer of Discovery Channel's Line of Fire and Weapons of War and BBC's Both Sides of the Line. Long experience and strong editorial control gives the military history enthusiast the ability to buy with confidence.

The series advisor is David McWhinnie, producer of the acclaimed Battlefield series for Discovery Channel. David and Bob have co-produced books and films with a wide variety of the UK's leading historians including Professor John Erickson and Dr David Chandler. Where possible the books draw on rare primary sources to give the military enthusiast new insights into a fascinating subject.

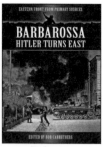
Barbarossa

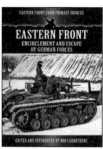
Eastern Front: Encirclement

Götterdämmerung

Eastern Front: Night Combat

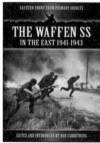
The Waffen SS in the East 1941-1943

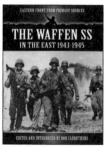
The Waffen SS in the East 1943-1945

The Wehrmacht Experience in Russia

Winter Warfare

The Red Army in Combat

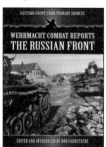
Wehrmacht Combat Reports: The Russian Front

For more information visit www.pen-and-sword.co.uk